MW00476914

"Mike's chemistry with his team systematically built my case allowing a jury to walk in my shoes and help them understand my mindset during the incident. Mike's understanding of the law, humble heart, and years of experience has earned him the highest respect among judges, attorneys, and experts nationwide."

—Nick Downey, *People v. Nick Downey* (The "horse thief" case)

"I could not have asked for a greater person to fight for my defense in the courtroom. Through the hundreds of hours researching and preparation to the days and weeks inside the courtroom, I was always comforted to know that I had Michael Schwartz in my corner. He consistently proved his reputation and record to be an accurate and a true representation of his skills as a litigator and his character as a human being. His book is a must read for any lawyer in trial practice!"

—Chad Jensen, *The United States of America v. Chad Jensen*

"My case was highly complex due to video evidence of the incident and multiple medical experts weighing in on the cause of death. The prosecution called no less than 3 separate high profile medical experts to present their conclusions. Under cross-examination, Michael was able to disprove their testimony by methodically debunking their conclusions one question at a time. I truly believe that because of Michael Schwartz, I received a 'not guilty' verdict within hours of deliberation after an almost two-month trial. Michael's honesty and professionalism are what make him stand out as a top-tier member of his profession. I can't imagine a better person to write a book on trial strategy!"

—Jay Cicinelli, *People v. Jay Patrick Cicinelli*
(The Kelly Thomas Murder Trial)

"Michael Schwartz did not have the easiest facts to deal with and still won. I knew from the start it was a very tough case. His approach was elegant yet dominant. Before trial ended and based on what my family saw, my family was so sure that Michael had 'sealed the deal' and that I was in good hands. They kept telling me, 'May the Schwartz be with you!' This book should be like the Bible for any trial attorney!"

—Chuck Holloway, *People v. Charles Holloway*

TRIAL AND THE **ART** OF *Sailing*

A Guidebook for New (and not so new) Attorneys to Navigate Trial Advocacy, and Life

MICHAEL D. SCHWARTZ

gatekeeper press
Columbus, Ohio

TRIAL AND THE ART OF SAILING
*A Guidebook for New (and Not So New) Attorneys
to Navigate Trial Advocacy, and Life*

Published by Gatekeeper Press
2167 Stringtown Rd, Suite 109
Columbus, OH 43123-2989
www.GatekeeperPress.com

Library of Congress Control Number: 2022948682

ISBN (hardcover): 9781662931239
ISBN (paperback): 9781662931246
eISBN: 9781662931253

Cover Art: Tzipporah Schwartz
Author Photo: Nathan Taylor Photography

With Thanks to The Almighty, Always . . .

For my wife:
My sounding board, mock juror, partner, and love,
with whom I've navigated life for the past twenty-two years . . .
Thank you.

CONTENTS

ACKNOWLEDGMENTS

No man is an island entire of itself . . .
—JOHN DONNE

Although there are always so many people who influence and help us in life, with regards to my career and this book, I'd like to thank and specifically acknowledge the following people:

My parents, Dr. Edward H. Schwartz, o"h, and my mom, Mrs. Sherry Schwartz, for a life full of love and support.

Mrs. Sandy Horn, my high school English teacher, mentor, and friend who once said that if I ever became a lawyer I'd settle for no less than becoming a hotshot trial lawyer (well, at the least the trial attorney part came true!).

Dr. Bernard Firestone of Hofstra University, who first advised me to pursue law school.

Mr. Ed Shacklee and Mrs. Lois Coon, my supervisors for my third-year law school criminal defense clinic, for their mentorship, instruction, and friendship.

The Honorable Zinora Mitchell-Rankin (Ret.), and the Honorable Michael Rankin (Ret.), for their mentorship, instruction, and influence on my then-budding career.

Mrs. Gail Evans (Leung), Esq. who supervised me at the San Francisco D.A.'s office, and allowed me a quiet, supportive environment to study, and pass the bar.

Mr. V. Roy Lefcourt, Esq., for his mentorship, instruction and friendship on my then-budding career.

Mr. Ken Clayman, The Public Defender for the County of Ventura (Ret.), for giving me my first full-time job as a lawyer, and the opportunity to grow into the attorney I've become.

Mr. Howard Asher, Esq., for his mentorship, instruction, and friendship in the early stages of my career.

Mr. Bruce Freed, Esq., for his mentorship, instruction, and friendship in the early stages of my career.

Mr. Nick Falcone, Esq., for his friendship, instruction, and mentorship in the early stages of my career.

Mr. Bob Willey, Esq., may he rest in peace, Assistant Public Defender for the County of Riverside, California, for his mentorship, instruction, and friendship throughout my career.

Mr. Gary Windom, Esq., The Public Defender for the County of Riverside, California (Ret.), for his mentorship, instruction, and friendship throughout my career.

Mr. Jorge Alvarado, Chief Public Defender of the State of New Mexico (Ret.), for his friendship, instruction, and mentorship throughout my career.

Mr. Bill Hadden, Esq., my colleague and friend, for his professionalism, friendship and sounding board during my tenure with Silver Hadden & Silver, and Rains Lucia Stern St. Phalle & Silver.

Mr. Steve Silver, Esq., for first hiring me, and his support, professionalism, and friendship during my tenure at Silver Hadden and Silver.

Mr. Harry Stern, Esq., friend, colleague, and kindred spirit, for his professionalism, friendship, support and sounding board during my tenure with Rains Lucia Stern St. Phalle and Silver.

Mr. Michael Eisenberg, Esq., friend, colleague, and kindred spirit, for his friendship and confidence in pushing me to go out on my own which not only fueled my self-confidence but gave me the time to write this book.

Mr. Zach Lopes, Esq., for his help and friendship on cases we worked on together.

Ms. Nicole Pifari, Esq., for her help and friendship on cases we worked on together.

Ms. Nicole Castronovo, Esq., for her help and friendship on cases we worked on together.

Mr. Tom Crompton, Mr. Robert "Bobby Mac" McFarlane, Mr. Robert "Bobby" Dean, and Mr. Damian Stafford, for their friendship and help on my cases; four of the best investigators an attorney could ever work with.

Ms. Cheryl Mitchell, for her help and friendship on this book and in cases we've worked on over the years.

Ms. Muriel Mateer, for her help and friendship on this book and in cases we've worked on over the years.

All my clients over the years for their faith in me to zealously, and competently, represent them.

But the mere truth won't do. You must have a lawyer.

—CHARLES DICKENS,
BLEAK HOUSE

WHY SAILING?

A ship in harbor is safe, but that's not what ships are built for.

—JOHN SHEDD

The overwhelming majority of cases never go to trial. Most attorneys don't have a lot of actual trial experience, whether they're new or even seasoned litigators. Jury trials, then, can be just as intimidating for experienced attorneys as for newer ones.

They shouldn't be.

The summer between my second and third years of law school, I landed an internship in the San Francisco County DA's office. Having spent nearly all of my first twenty-eight years of life on the East Coast, a summer in California—especially San Francisco—seemed like a great time. Add a cross-country trip there and back, the internship seemed secondary by comparison.

It wasn't. The experience as a bar-certified law student litigating cases in court was exciting and career building. Yet, despite all the events of that summer—the in-court experience, the Bay Area itself, Rocky Mountains, "Big Sky Country," and everything in between, there's one memory from that internship that has stayed with me more than all the others thirty years later.

Will Maas was a seasoned deputy public defender at the time of my internship. Tall, with short, neatly combed hair, a blond-grayish trimmed mustache, and self-confident but not arrogant, he was a force to be reckoned with; or so I was told.

It was my second day "on the job." One of my supervisors, deputy DA Gail Leung, took me almost by the hand to watch attorneys litigating preliminary hearings. I'd been late submitting my paperwork to the California bar; I was still waiting on approval to be bar certified. As soon as I received bar approval, I'd be conducting drug possession and low-level felony preliminary hearings for the DA's office that summer under the tutelage of attorney supervisors, Gail being one of them.

We walked into court in the middle of a hearing. I can't remember who the prosecutor was, but sitting at the defense table next to his client was Will Maas. There was a cop on the witness stand testifying, being asked direct examination questions. A law clerk was whispering in Will's right ear; his client was feverishly whispering in his left. Will had a police report in front of him, outlining and highlighting it. To call it multitasking was an understatement. People speaking in both ears, report being outlined, witness testifying.

"Objection, foundation, 352."

"Sustained. Counsel, lay a foundation."

Just like that. Cop testifying. Law clerk whispering. Client ranting. Highlighting and outlining a report. And still, not only timely objecting, but sustained! I smirked, shook my head, and wondered if I'd ever be that good, that experienced, *that natural at being a trial attorney.*

You may be thinking at this point, two pages into an introduction, that such an anecdote seems relevant for a book on trial advocacy, but why sailing? Let me explain by reversing course several years.

At age twenty-four, I was a working stiff in Manhattan, renting a bedroom in a two-bedroom co-op in Queens that my buddy Joey owned (and lived in as well). We both had full-time jobs and plans to change gears the following year. It was May 1989. I'd planned on leaving broadcast television to go to law school; Joey was about to earn his bachelor's degree that summer (he was a single dad, raising his son little Joey, working full time, and going to school at night, long before online courses or "online" anything even existed) and next year start graduate school for engineering. The last thing we'd planned on was buying a boat. But when a friend of mine at work took me for a Sunday sail on his boat, then the following week on *his* friend's boat (which happened to be for sale), I was hooked. I was already an avid scuba diver making a weekend habit of diving every shipwreck I could find off the coast of Long Island and New Jersey. A sailboat would be icing on the cake.

Joey wasn't convinced. First, neither of us knew how to sail. Although we'd both grown up on the North Shore of Long Island around, near, and in the water, sailing wasn't a middle- or working-class sport. But I was hooked and, therefore, convinced that we could teach ourselves without much effort. He also wasn't keen on spending his tuition money on a boat. The "plan," I told him, was to go half on the boat, have it for a season, then sell it. Even if we took a small loss, it'd be worth it to have a boat for a season. Even more, I prodded, if we took a week with our buddies in the Caribbean at a Club Med or Sandals, we'd easily drop about $1,500 and that's only a week. If we were willing to drop that for a week of fun in the sun, why not for a whole season on the water? Our individual losses couldn't amount to more than that.

One nighttime sail, and he was hooked. A week later, we were anchoring our "new" boat in our mooring in Huntington Harbor. It was a twenty-four-foot Capri that slept five people in the cabin. It had a main sail, a jib, and even a spinnaker. We sailed it after work, driving out from Queens, on weekends, you name it; that season, every spare second was spent on that boat. I'd throw on my dive gear once a week and go underneath to clean the hull.

Then came the moment. Joey had a family reunion out on the North Fork of Long Island. One of his uncles had rented a big beach house for the weekend; the reunion would be that Sunday. Cousins, second cousins, grandparents, aunts, uncles, you name it—a large Irish-Catholic family finally gathering everyone together. Joey invited me, too, with the thought that we'd sail there. A twenty-three-mile sail heading east on the Long Island Sound?

Of course, I said yes.

The reunion was set for Sunday morning. We'd planned on heading out Saturday night. Everything was set: food, beer, my copy of *Moby Dick*, Joey's then-girlfriend, and his younger brother.

A nor'easter came in that Friday, with winds gusting up to almost fifty miles an hour and *a lot* of rain. It lasted into Saturday, then Saturday night. Waves were cresting about ten feet. We waited, and waited, and waited. Friends came to the dock for a beer, curious if we were dumb enough or drunk enough (or both) to throw caution to the wind and sail, storm or no storm.

Although we weren't that stupid (or drunk, yet), we were 24. That whole "invincibility" thing that goes with youth. So, at about one thirty in the morning when the rain had basically stopped and the winds had died down to only about 10–20 mph, we decided to go for it. White caps were still breaking at about 5–7 feet; the boat was built for 7–10 feet at most. The wind had shifted and was now blowing from the northwest. A 20-knot wind basically behind us, white caps in front of us, a full cooler of beer next to us. We untied from the mooring and set sail.

At first, we both worked the boat. But we'd started at 1:30 a.m. and, with the late hour and the beer, we were getting tired. We agreed on shifts. Joey took the first shift, tightening the main sail, manning the jib and the rudder. I went below with my book and got a couple more hours of sleep before coming back up to relieve him. It was about 4:00 a.m. I kept the main sail locked down—the position seemed perfect for the wind direction—took hold of the jib, the rudder, and looked ahead. By that time, we were completely on the Sound, out of sight of any land. Alone on the deck, open water, heading due east.

Light.

The eastern horizon began to subtly change from dark purple to a softer blue. Slowly, slightly, it got brighter. Dark aqua turning to a lighter, solid blue.

Starting out as a small, yellow-orange glimmer on the edge of the horizon, within minutes the light mushroomed into a perfectly round, fiery ball rising above the waves directly in front of me. I was alone on the deck, working the jib and the rudder, keeping the wind filling the sails, boat gliding along the water, hypnotized by the moment. Once it fully crested the horizon, the sun was as big as the whole sky.

"I'm sailing on the open water, into the sunrise!" I kept grinning to myself. I don't know to this day what was bigger—my smile or that huge yellow ball that had just begun glowing on the waves. "Thank you, G-d! I'm doing it! I'm sailing *into* the sunrise! *I'm doing it!*"

Two months earlier, I had never sailed in my life. Now I was manning the boat by myself on the open water, sailing into a sunrise.

They say that a boat's like a person, that when you buy a boat that already has a name attached to it, you shouldn't change it. Our boat had a name when we bought it.

Dreamweaver.

We didn't change it.

Sailing into a sunrise, manning the boat on my own. In that moment, the entire universe seemed to fit. In that moment, anything seemed possible. In that moment, I felt whole.

Connected.

Sometimes I think we live our entire lives just for those moments.

Trials are like rivers, bodies of water. Like the open water, they're teeming with life. Trials have a dynamic, an energy, and movement. You can direct it to a degree, but you also need to let it direct you. In sailing, you can't fight the wind, you need to harness it, go with it, *feel it*. There can be sandbars, currents, and hidden obstacles; sometimes you feel like you've lost the wind altogether.

But you haven't.

A lot of things can influence your speed, direction, and ability to reach your destination. But most of all, a sailor needs to develop a feel for sailing, for becoming part of the different influences yet remain separate.

To connect.

No one sails in a straight line. Whether occasionally tacking, jibbing, or just making the constant small adjustments needed to catch the wind and stay on course, it's never a direct straight line.

As true as it is in sailing, it's even more so in trial. Experience, knowing your way, mapping out your course—all these metaphors apply. Constant adjustments, quick decisions (we'll talk more about that when we discuss objections). It's about staying on course, even if that course is not a straight line. A trial is fluid, like a good sail. The judge, opposing counsel, the jury, witnesses, evidence . . .

You need to connect to it.

Watching Will Maas in action during that preliminary hearing, I was in awe of someone who was really at one with what he was engaged in. He was doing it. He was *fully connected*. At that time, as a soon-to-be third-year law student, I wondered if I would ever be at that level as a trial attorney, to be that connected.

To really be that "in the moment," *as an attorney*.

Now, thirty years and almost two hundred trials and tribulations later, this book, besides being a labor of love (and life), is, I hope, an answer to that question.

CHAPTER ONE

KNOW YOUR AUDIENCE

Experience is the name everyone gives to their mistakes.

—OSCAR WILDE

My oldest daughter had always been a good student. But in fifth grade, the year did not start out on course.[1] "She can't teach," she complained about her teacher. "Nobody gets what she's saying." My wife was sympathetic; I wasn't.

"So, you want to change schools?" I joked

"No!" was the resounding answer.

"What should we do, then?" I'd ask, with my New York smirk, shrugging my shoulders. "Take her out?"

"Aba!" was the usual, frustrated retort.[2] My wife would get annoyed too.

"She's a good student! I don't want her getting bad grades because of one teacher!"

---

1   All the stories and anecdotes in this book are from the author's perspective. Some of the names have been changed to protect the party's privacy.

2   Aba is Hebrew for "dad."

After a few weeks of this, my wife and I finally sat our daughter down. "Look," I said. "Maybe she isn't a good teacher. I really don't know, I'm not in your class. But I do know that this year she's *your* teacher, and she's not going anywhere, and neither are you! So you need to figure out a way to make her happy and do well on her tests."

"But Aba, it's impossible!"

"No," I smirked back. "It's not. It's just hard." Then I let her have it, the logical argument, the lawyer coming out. "I'll bet that there are girls in your class still getting good grades. They've figured out what this teacher wants. You need to, too."

"But it's not my fault that she's not a good teacher!" she shot back.

"It may not be your fault, but it *is* your problem!"[3] I responded. "In life, sometimes you'll have a difficult boss, client, customer, teacher, judge. Maybe a 'bad' jury. It happens. But that's your audience. That's who and what you need to deal with. You don't quit; you figure out a way to deal with it. To still succeed."

Now, let's rewind to my first semester in law school. I knew the material so well I found myself tutoring our study group. We'd all been good students in college and in high school. After all, it was the George Washington (GW) Law school, a top-twenty school. I felt I knew the material, and my scholastic career up until that point should have been a good indicator that if I felt that way, I must have aced the exams.

---

3   I got this line from an administrative law judge (ALJ) almost fifteen years ago. I was litigating the paramedics' license of a firefighter. The ALJ assigned to the pre-hearing settlement conference was trying to convey to my client the benefits of avoiding the risk of hearing and settling the case by admitting misconduct and having his license put on a form of probation for almost two years. Thing is, my client didn't think he'd done anything wrong (and neither did I, for that matter). The ALJ told a story of how when he was a kid growing up in Hawaiian Gardens, he'd been arrested along with some of his friends. His working-class father had to take off part of a day from work to pick him up from the police station. He was not happy. After minutes of silence in the car, sensing his father's brewing anger, the young teenager blurted out, "But dad, I didn't do anything, it's not my fault!" His father pulled the car over, parked, and looked him in the eye. "It may not be your fault, but now it's your problem. And you need to deal with it." I've never forgotten that story or its import (Oh, and in the end, we didn't settle the case; we won!).

I didn't. For the first time in my life my grades were mediocre. Devastated, I sought out a couple of my professors to both complain and inquire why I had gotten Cs, and not As. Their answers were consistent: both said that although I knew the material, I didn't reflect that on the test in the format or approach they were looking for. In effect, I'd been a good student all my life, but now I had to be a good *law* student! I thought this was ludicrous! If I knew the material, I knew the material. Wasn't this just an exercise of form over substance?

"No," were my law professors' retorts. "It's no different than when you graduate and actually practice law. Doesn't matter how well you know or try your case, represent your client. It's how well it goes over with your audience. You need to know your audience."

With that in mind . . .

You've worked up your case. Witnesses are interviewed, subpoenaed, on call. Document evidence is in the queue, both on the computer and in hard copy. You've got your closing argument pretty much done, or at least outlined, and some of the main slides on your PowerPoint are set to go. Opening statement? Done. Cross-exams? Either written out or outlined, depending on your experience level and style. Client's been prepped in case he or she needs or wants to testify. You have your sympathetic facts, and you've strategized how to deflate or at least deal with your bad facts.

All you need is those twelve people in the box, your verdict, your win.

Question: Where are you trying the case? Is your jurisdiction liberal? Conservative? Pro-employer? Pro-employee? Law and order? Who's your "victim?" Male? Female? His or her ethnicity? Race? How presentable is your client?

Get the picture? You might have a great case for San Francisco, but if you're trying the case in Victorville or Fresno, maybe you should rethink your approach.

How will the average juror in the jurisdiction you're *in* feel about your case, your client, *you*? And what about the judge you're in front of?

Is it state court or federal court?

The first, middle, and last factor to consider in trial work is knowing your audience. Your colleagues, your husband, your wife, boyfriend, girlfriend, or pet parrot will not be deciding your case. Those twelve people in the box (or the one behind the bench) will be. They're your audience.

Everyone else may be good sounding boards, devil's advocates, but at the end of the day, they're not your jury. And neither are you. The first thing to consider when strategizing, preparing, even in advising your client on the potential outcomes and viability of his or her case is who the audience will be and how well (or not) will your approach, theme, and evidence go over with that audience. At least generally. Once the jury is picked or you know which judge you're in front of, you can then try to get more specific in how and what evidence you'll present, when you'll present it, and how you litigate your case.

Sympathy vs. Empathy

Many attorneys fool themselves into thinking that their goal is to evoke sympathy for their clients from either the jury or judge (or both). They're wrong. Sympathy, although usually ascribed as a very positive trait, is overrated. As quickly as it comes, it goes. It doesn't last, so neither will that juror's allegiance to your argument. It's empathy that wins the day. In developing your theory of the case, remaining cognizant of your jurisdiction and potential audience, you need to build a presentation that instills empathy for your case and client in the minds and hearts of the jurors. Empathetic presentations win cases; sympathetic ones don't.

Don't Take Your Argument or Facts for Granted: Joanna

Each case or trial has its own unique challenges. I learned early on in my career that in trial work, regardless of how well you feel you litigated a case, the only opinions that really count are those of the twelve people in the jury box.

Back in the fall of 1996, I was a deputy public defender and somewhat new to felonies. Hired less than three years earlier, I already had well over a hundred misdemeanor jury trials under my belt. In Ventura County in the nineties, unless you really made an effort to avoid trial, you went to trial. It was a conservative county; the district attorney for over fifteen years was known for not settling cases. Felony cases, especially. If the judge couldn't (or wouldn't) give you a decent plea offer, as the saying goes, you just put twelve in the box and went to trial.

I was already making a name for myself in the courthouse. Although public defenders are "meant to lose" cases, I won most of mine. And I didn't cherry-pick either. Maybe I had a knack for trials, I thought at the time, or maybe a natural ability. Whatever it was, I had developed a reputation in my misdemeanor assignment as a formidable opponent, one who rarely lost.

I brought that attitude and swagger with me into my new felony assignment. Already being mentored by some experienced, talented, more senior attorneys, I'd been warned more than once, "Just wait until you get to felonies." Now, I was there. From the beginning, probably because of my lack of felony trial experience, it really seemed no different than misdemeanor court, only on steroids.

My wake-up call came with a domestic violence case I was assigned. My client, we'll call her "Joanna," was a Mexican woman around mid-thirties, heavyset, and very quiet. She was charged with two felonies: Domestic violence against her husband, and an assault with a deadly weapon, also against her husband. Basically, she stabbed him in the knee during a domestic dispute. Speaking to her through a translator, however, her story was "sympathetic."

Her husband was on two different misdemeanor probations for beating her. Scared of him, she still wouldn't leave him partly because she didn't want to break up the family (they had two small kids together), but mostly because he had threatened her that if she did leave, he'd have her deported. He had a green card, even with his misdemeanor convictions. Although she'd been in the United States most of her adult life, she didn't. It was an omission that he routinely held over her head. She stayed with him and suffered his bullying and beatings.

Until one night, when she couldn't take it anymore. She was washing the dishes. He had come home from being out and demanded dinner. It was late. He was drunk. She told him dinner had been a couple of hours ago when she'd expected him to be home. Remember, this was in the 1990s, before the prevalence of cell phones.

Joanna's husband got angry and started throwing things. Joanna told him to stop, which only made him angrier. He came toward her and gave her a smack. Then he turned around quickly and picked up a broomstick. He wasn't looking to sweep the floor. Scared at the prospect she'd get beaten again, this time with a wooden stick, Joanna grabbed the closest thing she could find to defend herself: a kitchen knife she'd just washed. He got closer. She lashed out, puncturing his knee. The wound was deep. Shocked, she grabbed her daughter who had just wandered into the middle of the melee and ran outside. She told a neighbor she'd just stabbed her husband, and he might need an ambulance. He limped out behind her. The police were called, as were the paramedics. Although he was treated and released the same night, the medical records indicated he'd lost a lot of blood. In effect, he'd almost bled out. On the way to the hospital, he gave a statement to the police, not much different than what Joanna had said.[4]

Joanna was arrested and charged with felony domestic violence and assault with a deadly weapon: two strikes.[5]

We thought we had a good case. Sympathetic client, unsympathetic "victim." Both of her husband's two prior domestic violence convictions came into evidence. The broomstick, the fear—it all came in. The husband tried to minimize his prior convictions on the stand, to minimize his actions that night. I impeached him with his own promises he'd made at the two prior sentencing hearings: that he wouldn't beat his wife again and that he'd act appropriately. Even more, one of his probation terms was that he could no longer consume alcohol! He looked like a liar—a bullying, brutish liar. The icing on the cake was his admission on the way to the hospital of hitting her before she stabbed him. He claimed to have picked up the

---

4   He had used the word "tortazo" in describing the smack he'd given his wife. Tortazo can mean a "smack," which is how the court-certified interpreter translated it for the prosecution's transcript of his statement. Even my own Spanish-speaking investigator defined it similarly. But in other contexts, it can mean a real "wallop." Problem was, we came to find that out too late; it wasn't until after the trial, in a casual conversation with a different court interpreter, that we found out it could mean either a slap in the face or a really hard blow.

5   In California, certain serious felonies are called "strikes," carrying with them, upon conviction, a presumption of a state prison sentence instead of probation. Additionally, if a person reoffended, it ratcheted up their sentence, doubling it. If a person suffered two strike convictions, any felony conviction, be it a strike or not, would be a "third strike," mandating a life sentence in prison.

broomstick after he saw her grab a knife. I thought it didn't matter—she'd grabbed the knife after he'd hit her! And he had a history of hitting her!

In closing argument, I hammered home the self-defense instruction to the jury, waxed poetic about battered women, called him the liar and abuser I felt (and thought everyone else did, by that point) he was. The jury went back to deliberate, and the judge congratulated me on my argument and my case. So did the bailiff, the court clerk, and the court reporter. Even the deputy DA shook my hand and said he knew he'd had a tough case, but hey, he had his marching orders, and at least the jury would do the right thing.

They didn't. Joanna was convicted of both counts.

I was floored. We spoke to the jury afterward. They were "sympathetic." Some even said they "had a doubt," but they couldn't get past the knife to the knee, the bleeding, and the child in the room. They said that a knife was a deadly weapon, a broomstick wasn't. But hadn't I gone over that in the closing argument? That was all part of the self-defense instruction, that the force a person uses to defend herself does *not* have to equal the force she was facing from the aggressor. And a broomstick can definitely cause serious bodily injury! What about her husband's prior convictions for domestic violence? The *tortazo*?

Didn't matter. The jurors felt she shouldn't have picked up the knife. End of story.

The deputy DA argued at sentencing that Joanna should reasonably go to prison (even though, personally, he had thought the jury should have acquitted her) because she'd been convicted of two serious felonies, but in light of her not having a record, probation and one year in jail was fitting. Again, the good soldier.[6]

The judge bent over backward to be lenient at sentencing, granting her probation, no jail time, and promising that at the end of probation he'd lower the convictions to misdemeanors. Joanna was very appreciative of all our efforts.

---

6   To his credit, that same deputy DA left the office and went into the private sector where he wouldn't be compromising his conscience to play the good soldier. Some district attorney offices give their trial deputies discretion on cases. In the 1990s, Ventura was not one of them.

For my part, I was still upset. At the jurors, at the translator, but mostly at myself. How could I have lost that trial? Maybe I wasn't cut out for felonies? Seemed so simple, so cut and dry. The judge thought I'd won. The clerk, the bailiff, even the prosecutor.

But not those twelve people in the box. Although at that point in my career I had litigated over a hundred jury trials, the overwhelming majority were misdemeanors, which meant not only were the stakes lower, but the conduct and injuries were also less serious. Two things I learned from that trial:

1. I needed to adjust not only my approach for felony cases, but my entire thought process. In a misdemeanor case, though the outcome can impact your client immensely, the stakes are relatively low for society. It's much easier for people to give the benefit of the doubt to someone charged with stealing $25 worth of CDs or pushing his wife or her husband. If the jury is wrong, it's not like they're letting Ted Bundy go free. But in a felony case, if the jury is wrong, they may subconsciously (or even outwardly) worry about letting a real felon walk away, back into society. That fear, real or imagined, is influential. It needs to be addressed by the attorney, either in influencing his or her entire approach to the case, in *voir dire*, or both.

2. I was still practicing law in a very conservative jurisdiction. Though the laws for battered women may have changed after the O.J. Simpson case, the jurors' attitudes in conservative Ventura County hadn't. My client, though a battered woman, was still a criminal defendant. I relied too heavily on my own personal bias in the case. To me, it was obvious she was a victim. But to a conservative, prosecution-oriented jury, she was the defendant. I needed to humanize her more, and it should've begun if not in voir dire, then in a much more detailed, heartfelt (toeing the line between fact and argument) opening statement.[7] My personal views and feelings clouded my presentation and expectations. I had forgotten my audience.

One of the goals of a trial attorney is to get the jury to *empathize* with his client, not sympathize.

Empathize.

---

7   We'll talk more about what to consider when deciding how detailed to make your opening statement, and ways to walk that line between fact and argument, in Chapter 9.

Jury Dynamics—Jury Personalities

Speaking to the jurors after that trial, I began to realize that there are, generally, several different kinds of jurors in the world, with obvious variations within the three categories I'm about to describe:

Self-absorbed. Self-absorbed people can range from the socio-pathic to someone who simply lives the "me" mentality. They're not necessarily selfish. Self-absorbed means nothing really exists for them outside of their own personal thoughts, feelings, and experiences. When it goes too far to the extreme, it becomes sociopathic. We've all heard of or experienced them: people who can rationalize any behavior. The worst of the worst usually come to mind: Hitler, Stalin, Jeffrey Dahmer. People who can act with the most monstrous of intent with no remorse. The other end of that spectrum are people who, obviously, aren't monstrous but have a hard time seeing the world outside of their own personal fishbowl. Again, they're never wrong, but routinely "wronged." Their world (and everyone else's in their lives, at least in their minds) usually revolves around them. Although not impossible, it's more than difficult to get someone like this to empathize with your client or your case unless they're already predisposed to that position.

Sympathetic. Before you had read the introductory paragraph to this chapter, you probably thought that what you want on your jury are sympathetic people. And, unless that self-absorbed juror you left on your jury is predisposed to your case, sympathetic people are better than self-absorbed people. But you're probably also thinking that I'm being way too general and, consequently, unfair. Judgmental. Someone can be self-absorbed, or at least have some self-absorbed tendencies, and still be a sympathetic person, right? Not every person who has some self-absorption is a sociopath.

That's right, they're not. And I did qualify my comments about the different categories—that there would be variations within all three. We're only up to number two. But a huge part of jury selection (which we'll discuss in more detail in Chapter 9, Voir Dire) is based on ste-reotyping and generalizing. It needs to be. You really don't get much information about your prospective jurors (i.e., your audience) before they *become* your audience. Generalities and stereotypes are, unfortunately, tools of the trade in trial work, albeit always with a grain of salt.

Yes, sympathetic people are preferable to self-absorbed people. But to be blunt, being able to have sympathy for another human being isn't the definition of a good person or a caring human being. If a person can't feel at least a moment of sympathy for another person's plight, then we need to wonder if he's really just Joseph Stalin in sheep's clothing. Sympathy is momentary; it's a baseline—a watermark that we're human. It's that quick feeling of compassion a person has for another human being. But it's fleeting. As quickly as it comes, it can go. It leaves no lasting impression on a person. It makes us human, sure, but not necessarily a real, caring human. That's why even a self-absorbed person can have sympathy for someone else—take a moment, feel badly, and then move on, back to *me* and *my* life.

So, if we obviously don't want a fanatically self-absorbed serial killer on our jury, and a sympathetic person isn't the ultimate juror, who is?

Empathetic. Empathy differs from sympathy in one significant way: empathetic people *feel* the other person's pain, not just intellectually, but also emotionally. They can put themselves in someone else's shoes. As an advocate, you're not trying to elicit sympathy for your client and your case. Again, it's fleeting. As quickly as your jury feels for you and your client, they can be easily persuaded to feel for the other side. The key, then, is to try to figure out which jurors are empathetic people as well as trying to help those "sympathetic" jurors become empathetic. A mistake many attorneys make is assuming that because the attorney and her small circle of confidants are empathetic to her client's case, the jury will be too.

WRONG.

I made that mistake in Joanna's case. I didn't focus on instilling *empathy* in the jury for Joanna and her situation. I didn't do a good enough job directing the jurors' emotions on how sincerely scared and intimidated they would feel if they were in her shoes.

I simply showed them the shoes.

And I lost.

Judges Are People Too

"Jill Jones" was a vivacious person—a member of a four-woman traveling chorus for her church, participating with her husband in community projects, raising three children. Then one morning, she called out in pain to her husband. Jill had suffered a debilitating brain aneurysm. This once vivacious woman was now in a coma.

In Jill's third week after she came out of the coma, I met "Rick," Jill's husband, through a mutual friend. He was living in a trailer in the parking lot of the hospice where Jill was convalescing. She was paralyzed, and barely able to speak or make sounds. But she was alert. Rick and I became fast friends. I started making weekly visits to him and Jill.

After about six months convalescing, Jill came home. She was now in a wheelchair, unable to walk or care for herself. Her speech was also affected—once part of a traveling quartet, it was now a challenge just to put together a sentence. Rick, a naturally positive person, did his best to keep the house, go to work, and finish raising his now young-adult kids.

"Bobby," the Joneses' son, was very close to his mom. Her energy, optimism, vitality. To see her now resigned to a wheelchair not able to care for herself and barely able to speak destroyed him emotionally. He was devastated. A once successful college student, he was barely attending classes. He spent his time self-medicating by smoking as much pot as he could and vegetating in his father's trailer, which, having left the parking lot of the hospice, was now parked in Rick's backyard. Months of this downward spiral led to suicidal thoughts. He grew his hair long, rarely showered, and began to look like the recluse he was evolving into. Still reeling from Jill's aneurysm and current condition, watching Bobby deteriorate in front of their eyes caused the family that much more anguish.

Rick and Jill's neighbor was a middle-aged woman about the same age as Jill. "Cindy" lived by herself and had always been friendly with the Joneses. The Jones kids would help her with her yardwork, exchange pleasantries, and, when they were younger, be invited over for cookies. Not necessarily the best of friends, but good neighbors nonetheless.

One Tuesday afternoon, Bobby's desperation hit a peak. He first went into the street and lay down, hoping a passing car would run him over. A few minutes passed before he realized that any car driving on a residential street would most likely swerve and miss him or, at best, hit him to cause harm, but not death. He got up and looked next door. Cindy's car wasn't there. He remembered she owned a gun. Assuming she wasn't home, he figured he could break in, find the gun, and put an end to his desperation. He went around the back of the house, found the screen door closed but the back door unlocked. He turned the handle and went inside.

He figured she was a middle-aged single woman, so the gun would probably be in her bedroom, probably on or in a nightstand for easy access. He knew where her bedroom was because he'd helped her move some furniture a few years earlier. He walked through the kitchen, turned right down the hallway, and entered her bedroom.

Cindy was home (she had had eye surgery that morning and left her car with a friend.). She lay on her bed, wet compacts on her recovering eyes. Hearing the intruder obviously startled her. She sat up, and the cold compresses fell off her face. Her vision still somewhat blurry from the morning's surgery, she could make out only a fuzzy image of a long-haired, disheveled man coming toward her.

She jumped out of bed, screaming.

Bobby, surprised to find her home and startled by her reaction, screamed too. He stretched out his arms to hug this surrogate mother figure who he'd grown up with, sometimes yelling, sometimes almost whispering, "Please, just come here! I want you!" He tried to hug her; she pushed him away, ran out of her room and down the hall, nearly falling out her back door. Scared, her vision still blurry, she would later testify that she was sure he'd come to rape her, and only her knowledge of the layout of her home where she'd lived for twenty years allowed her to make her way down the hall and outside.

Bobby, convinced that he could persuade Cindy of his good intentions, ran after her, down the hallway, out the back door. He chased her around the backyard, all the while Cindy was screaming for help, for the police, while Bobby was yelling for her to come to him, to hug him. She made her way onto the front lawn where a neighbor from across the street took her in. Seeing that she'd gone, Bobby retired to his trailer and packed a bong. He'd failed in killing himself. He'd failed in procuring some physical affection from a mother figure. Time to self-medicate. The episode was over.

Or so he thought.

A few hours later there was a knock on the trailer door. Two detectives wanted to talk to Bobby. He invited them in, and the three of them began a conversation. The trailer was small; the detectives would later testify that it reeked like marijuana. Bobby sat on one side of the small table that he used for his meals; one detective sat across from him, one next to him. They started with small talk, and slowly segued into what had happened earlier in the day. When one of the detectives began to casually tell Bobby about his Miranda rights, Bobby asked if they were police officers or psychologists. The detectives told Bobby they were there to help him, that they could see he was a "troubled young man," and he'd feel better if he just confided in them what had happened. Stoned, tired, and emotionally unstable Bobby again asked the detectives if they were psychologists. One of them laughed and said that he'd been doing this for long enough and spoke to enough troubled people that he probably could pass for a psychologist. Bobby then admitted to entering the house without permission and chasing after Cindy. He told them he'd "broken in" to "take her gun" and kill himself. When he saw her on the bed, he only wanted "some love, something physical."

The detectives arrested Bobby. He was charged with one count of a residential burglary and one count of assault with the intent to commit rape. Two serious felonies. Two strikes.[8]

Upon his son's arrest, Rick immediately called me. I was a deputy public defender at the time and had been assigned to felony trials for only a couple of years. In my misdemeanor assignment and for those first two years in felonies, I had developed a reputation as a "trial hound," and a very good one. I'd been a deputy public defender, actually a lawyer, for only about four years. I'd already litigated close to one hundred fifty jury trials to verdict with positive results. Rick asked, almost pleaded with me, to take his son's case. A mutual friend of ours, a private attorney, had offered. But even with a huge discount, Rick and Jill couldn't afford it due to her ongoing medical expenses, their other kids' needs, and becoming a single-income family.

---

8 In the California penal code, certain enumerated felonies are considered "strikes." If a person is convicted of three felonies in his or her lifetime and the first two of those three are "strikes," the person can be sentenced to life in prison for the third felony, even though it is not a strike or even a serious felony. Bobby's future, then, had turned very bleak.

Bobby's defense was in my office's hands. Rick, a close friend, begged me to put his son's future in *my* hands.

Against my better judgment, I finally capitulated. It was almost the emotional mistake of my career.

Bobby, having gone back and forth with suicidal thoughts before the incident, was diagnosed as a paranoid schizophrenic and medicated while in custody. Heavily medicated. His hair remained long and unkempt. I had known him as a young, troubled college student from a good family who had a hard time dealing with his mother's tragedy. He now looked and presented like Charles Manson without the beard. I did not want to put him in front of a jury.

The prosecutor was young, ambitious. While sympathizing to a degree, he also had to walk his office's party line. As I stated above, at that time the Ventura County district attorney had a policy: no plea bargains on Prop 8 cases (serious felonies). If we were to try to cut a deal, Bobby would have to plead guilty to two strikes. In his condition, the likelihood that he may reoffend in the future was more than a possibility. A new felony offense, even a minor one like drug possession, would mean life in prison. The only real choice was trial.

The case wound its way to preliminary hearing. The prosecutor decided to put on a Prop 115 hearing.[9] The lead detective testified to the facts in his police report. Cindy did not testify.

After the prosecution case, the judge, Charles McGrath, held Bobby to answer, meaning there was enough evidence that the case could go forward to trial. I had expected that. There was a saying among defense attorneys that if the prosecutor put a ham sandwich on the stand, your client would be held to answer.

But while doing so, the judge made a comment: "While I am holding the defendant to answer based on this evidence, this is a probable cause

---

9   California Proposition 115, among other things, allowed that police officers who either had five years or more experience as a sworn officer, or were "Prop 115 certified" through a course at their initial police academy could testify to hearsay (out of court statements by other witnesses) at preliminary hearings, obviating the need for the prosecution to put on alleged victims or other "live witnesses" at the hearing, which worked to facilitate hearings being litigated more quickly.

hearing and the standard is, then, well below that of proof beyond a reasonable doubt at trial. The prosecution may want to take another look at this."

I was stunned with hope! He got it, I smiled to myself. This judge got it!

Three weeks later the DA's office filed two serious felonies in superior court—the residential burglary and the assault with intent to commit rape. We pled not guilty, and the case was set for trial. I'd asked a few of the more senior attorneys in the office about the judge I'd had for the preliminary hearing. They all said he was one of the better superior court judges in the building. We all agreed if, with G-d's help, I could somehow maneuver the case back in front of him for trial, it was worth waiving jury trial and having a court trial, based both on his reputation and what he'd said as part of his holding order. I continued the case a few times, keeping track of when he'd be available for our trial.

The judge in the master calendar court at the time respected and liked me. The morning Judge McGrath's courtroom opened up for assignment, we announced ready for trial. The master calendar judge called me and the prosecutor to the bench. "I have two courtrooms available, Judge Klopfer and Judge McGrath." The judge looked at me and smirked. "Is there a preference?" I had to think. Judge Klopfer also liked and respected me—I'd gotten a child abuse case in front of him dismissed mid-trial after my cross-exam of the alleged victim. He'd even granted my motion for a factual finding of innocence, which is never granted. But McGrath had a good reputation, and *he had made those comments at the preliminary hearing.*

I looked at the prosecutor. "Either is fine with me," I feigned, "but Judge McGrath did hear the prelim and is familiar with some of the issues. Might be good to not have to reinvent the wheel." In reality, we wouldn't be "reinventing" anything; preliminary hearings rarely have issues, and even more rare are issues that impact trials. In this case, the impact would be zero. The deputy DA really didn't care where we were sent and acquiesced to McGrath. Inside, I was ecstatic; I thought Bobby now had a shot at getting acquitted.

I then suggested to the prosecutor that we waive jury trial and opt for a court trial. Quicker, easier. To say it's rare for a defense attorney, especially in such a conservative jurisdiction like Ventura County, to waive his client's right to a trial by jury is like saying it's rare for it to snow in Death Valley. It just didn't happen. But again, I was maneuvering the case to where I wanted it. Judge McGrath was not impressed with the evidence at preliminary hearing. Trial was a higher standard. The prosecutor would have to prove his case beyond a reasonable doubt by the close of the trial. The defense had a psychologist on board to rebut intent in case the prosecution was able to meet that burden.

Everything was going according to plan.

What I didn't plan on was how empathetic Cindy would be on the witness stand. To this day I sincerely believe that *she* truly believed, albeit erroneously, that Bobby wanted to rape her. The contrasting images were striking. Cindy crying, shaking, still scared on the witness stand—a middle-aged, slender, intelligent, soft-spoken woman. Bobby sitting at the defense table—long, unkempt hair, glassy eyes, and dropped-open jaw from his medication. At least outwardly he presented as the monster she was describing. We put on the psychologist in our case-in-chief, who described Bobby's slow deterioration, his need for a mother figure, his need for physical affection from that maternal figure. Judge McGrath listened attentively and took copious notes.

Then he convicted him of both counts.

I was devastated. Rick could not afford to take off from work. Bobby's sister was in the courtroom for the judge's verdict. Teary-eyed, she graciously thanked me for trying and asked what was next. My voice cracked. "The judge will want a probation report. And then sentencing." Fighting back tears, she continued, "Will he go to prison?"

"I don't know," was all I could answer. When I got back to my office, there was already a message from Rick on my voice mail. He was equally gracious. "Michael, I know you tried your hardest. I just want to thank you for everything. The system is what it is."

In the end, waiving jury was still the right decision. Judge McGrath didn't sentence Bobby to prison. Instead, he granted him probation and sentenced him to a year in a halfway house for people battling mental health issues, with a six-month review and the potential for early release. Bobby did suffer two strikes on his record. One more mistake, however minor, a felony would put him in prison for life. I went to my supervisor and asked for some R&R from felony trials. I was reassigned to juvenile court for a year of "rest."

Lesson learned: judges are people too. Regardless of a judge's reputation and comments at a hearing, a trial—even a court trial—is a different setting altogether. Sure, the standard of proof is drastically different, which, if you think about it, should have inured in my favor. But the stakes are also higher, and the evidence most of the time has a different flavor to it, even if it is "almost exactly" the same, *because* the stakes are higher. We don't decide our own cases. Sounds basic, but it's easily forgotten. Judges may be more experienced in litigation than the average juror, and many times more tainted, but they are always just as human.[10] Which means they're influenced by appearances, experiences, emotions.[11]

---

10 I'd waived jury on another felony trial in Ventura about a year earlier. The long/short of it: My client was diagnosed as a paranoid schizophrenic in that case, too, and had led the Simi Valley police, CHP, and eventually the LAPD on a long, low-speed 45-mile chase from Simi Valley into a bus depot in LA, where after a few minutes of cat and mouse with the officers he collided with a Simi Valley unit, causing some damage to the car and minor injury to the officer. He was charged with a felony evading arrest and a felony assault with a deadly weapon (California Penal Code section 245) for the vehicle collision. We pled to the evading but went to trial on the 245 charge. We waived jury. I had a full-scale model of the bus depot, buses, and police cars made for the trial. During one of the officers' testimony and closing arguments, the judge asked if he could come off the bench and "check out" the model. He moved cars around, re-positioned them and put them back. Not once, not twice, but over and over again. We ended up beating the 245! Our office used to joke afterward that if you're going to waive jury, you'd better have something for the judge to play with!

11 There was another judge back in my Ventura days who I had also litigated and won a few trials in his court, so he respected me. The more I won, the more he respected me and treated me well. Although it was obvious that he liked me, he had a mental block pronouncing my name. "Schwartz" is pronounced "Sh," like "shells." He pronounced it "S" like "sea." "Mr. Swartz" was my name in front of juries when introducing me. "Mr. Swartz" was my name whenever he addressed me. For some reason, it annoyed me. I corrected him subtly, but nothing helped.

Then one trial, before jury selection, the prosecutor and I were in chambers with the judge, discussing pre-trial issues. The judge kept referring to me as "Mr. Swartz." Finally, in front of the prosecutor, I looked across the judge's desk and said, "Your Honor, the court knows I respect the court and we actually get along well. But for years the court has mispronounced my name. It's "Schwartz," not "Swartz."

"Swartz?" he asked again, actually sincerely.

I smirked. "Your honor, let me be blunt. When the court goes to the bathroom, does the court take a "sit," or take a—"

He interrupted me, his face turning red and smiled, "I understand, Mr. Schwartz." When you know your audience, you know your audience.

Most of us want to think we're in control. Many of the people who gravitate to litigation and trial work operate under the delusion that we can control the outcome of our cases. Influence, yes. Control, no. We manipulate, plan, strategize, plot, and execute. Trial work is a game of chess. We think that if we can simply best our opponent, we win. In reality, however, although we do have to try our best to "best" the other side by thinking and planning one, two, or three steps ahead, we don't decide the outcome. And that's a point I'm going to come back to more than once. To believe otherwise can break the emotional and, by derivation, overall career of very talented people. All we can really do is try our best. We decide how much effort, thought, and how much of ourselves we put into a case. Our experience plays a vital role, as does our preparation and determination. Some of us become masters at thinking on our feet or rolling with the evidence. But we're not in charge of the final result. Once that is not only understood but digested, incorporated, and ingrained into your psyche, you can have a career, hopefully a successful one, as a trial attorney.

An attorney can try a great case, even have what appear to be sympathetic facts. But at the end of the day, we're not in charge of the outcome. My faith tells me that the outcome is in the hands of G-d, through whatever means we're dealing with—be it a jury, judge, or arbitrator. For those who do not hold that same belief, suffice it to say that at the very least, no one can definitively alter or read the mind of a juror, let alone twelve of them. And we haven't even spoken about the added dynamic of how those twelve strangers interact with and influence each other behind closed doors. All you can do is give it your best effort. Never forget that.

I started my book describing two losses. Doesn't really invoke a lot of confidence in the reader looking to learn from a professed trial guru all about trial work, does it?

Well, first off, I'm not a trial guru, just an attorney whose been blessed with a lot of trial experience and a good track record. Second, people always tend to second-guess losses and to build on them. You learn much more from mistakes and failures/losses than you do from victories (probably because we rarely scrutinize our victories). Looking back, Bobby's case taught me to not grab on too tightly to any positive fact or development, be it a judge's comment or a piece of evidence. It also served as a lasting reminder that everyone in the system is human and will act that way. That may sound obvious, but we tend to ascribe superhuman or otherworldly qualities to those whom we respect and admire, just to watch our own expectations come crashing down when the cracks in the marble pedestals we've put them on become patently noticeable. It happens in court; it happens in life. Don't let it happen to you.

Bobby's case also taught me that as much as the judge seemed to sympathize with our case at the preliminary hearing, that was before he saw Cindy testify. Judge McGrath was at the time probably in his mid-to-late fifties, had a wife probably not much older than Cindy, kids not much younger. He could identify more with Cindy's fear than Bobby's desperation. He sympathized with us at the preliminary hearing. He empathized with Cindy at trial.

Sympathy vs. empathy.

Empathy won.

Joanna's case helped me not only in ways already described, but also years later—when my niche would evolve into defending police officers in high-profile cases involving uses of force and officer-involved shootings—to better understand and explain the principles of self-defense. The verdict in Joanna's case taught me to double down on the principle that when a person is defending himself or herself from an imminent threat, he or she need not use the same force that the aggressor is threatening them with but can and, common sense dictates, needs to use greater force to neutralize that threat. Joanna's jury didn't digest that fully; it was my fault. I took my facts and how I viewed them for granted. Again, although the jury sympathized with Joanna, they didn't empathize with her.

This book will flip back and forth between blunt advice, mistakes lived and learned, anecdotes, war stories, and, believe it or not, good old-fashioned common sense. It's been my experience that people don't learn much by being spoken or lectured to, which makes writing a book a bit of a challenge. In reading this, it'll hopefully feel less like a lecture and more like a conversation, or a friend advising a colleague.

KNOW YOUR AUDIENCE
Compass Points

• • •

A. **Your presentation needs to be geared toward your audience, for example:**
   - conservative or liberal
   - cosmopolitan or more suburban
   - race
   - age
   - gender

B. **Don't take your argument or facts for granted.**
   - Jury personalities
     - ✓ *self-absorbed*
     - ✓ *sympathetic*
     - ✓ *empathetic*
   - Understand that how you see your client may not be how the jury or judge will see your client (e.g., Bobby's case).
   - Evoke empathy, not just sympathy, in your audience.

CHAPTER TWO

CLOSING ARGUMENT

The beginning is wedged in the end, and
the end is wedged in the beginning.
—HASIDIC SAYING

You might be asking, as we begin to teach about trial advocacy, shouldn't we be starting with voir dire? After all, it's the beginning of every jury trial. It comes first. Right?

There's a Hasidic saying about life and the cosmos: "The beginning is wedged in the end, and the end is wedged in the beginning." Nothing could be more true of jury trials.

I was taught at the start of my career, and it's my still practice (although I've varied the form and personalized the approach over the years) that when you begin to prepare a case, start to articulate or outline your closing argument from the get-go. That's right, your *closing* argument. Because it's what you plan to argue that guides you in how to approach, prepare, strategize, and finally litigate your case. Some call it their "theory" of the case. Some, the story, the narrative. The label makes no difference.

The Elements—Jury Instructions

First, look up the elements the prosecution needs to prove. If you're a plaintiff attorney, just approach it from the mirror image—what elements do I need to prove? Best place to look is not in the statute or code, but in the jury instructions (if there are standard instructions for that particular offense or cause of action) because that's what the jury will be working with come the end of the case.

The jury instructions direct how you argue your case in the end, so they should direct how you approach your case in the beginning.

Based on those elements, you can then look at the evidence, at least what you know so far or expect or reasonably hope it to be. What evidence do you know of right now that either fits into your theory of the case or works against it? What evidence do you need, if any, to rebut the other side's case or strengthen or prove yours? How would you then weave that evidence into the specific elements or defense?

You now have the beginning of an outline for your closing argument.

If you do this exercise and come back to it as the case progresses— be it through the discovery process, investigative process, witness preparation, and evidentiary preparation—it will not only focus your eventual closing argument but also help direct your strategy in the organization and planning of the case itself. It'll keep you on track. And one more benefit: You'll begin to articulate the facts and arguments both in your mind and out loud enough times that by the time you get to the closing argument, some, if not all, will roll off your tongue. The elements are the heart of the case, whether you're proving them or defending against that "proof." Always having them in mind keeps your eye on the proverbial ball.

Start Looking at Big Points First

There are two ways of approaching life: big picture and little picture. Big picture means grand ideas, themes, what the puzzle is supposed to look like as a whole in the end. People who approach life this way are the dreamers, "idea" people, visionaries.

Little picture represents the nuts and bolts, the details, even what seem to be the most minor, mundane details. What's in front of me right now. *What do I have to do?* People with this approach to life are usually detail-oriented, generally great at working on a project, and can get completely wrapped up in the present. They thrive on the minutiae.

Yes, some people are more "big picture" oriented, some more "little picture" oriented. In trial work, like in life, the optimal approach is to marry the two, i.e., to always have big picture in mind, to know where you want to go and then constantly fit little picture into big picture, which are the nuts and bolts on how to get there. Looking at the big points first—the elements—and then little picture— those pieces of evidence that naturally speak to those elements (to either prove or defend against them)—is how you begin the exercise of big picture/little picture. It will keep you focused.

A few years ago, my wife, a trained fashion designer (before we got married and she devoted herself to raising our kids), took up painting. She had always talked about her dream to paint. I'd seen her fashion portfolio over the years; she was talented. She'd even begun her own line in France before we met. To me, the creativity and gifts were there. All she was lacking was experience and, even more, the self-confidence that comes with experience.[12] So one Mother's Day, rather than get her flowers, I took her to a local art supply store and bought her a few canvases, brushes, and paint. Acrylic paint, because she felt that oils were too expensive to "waste" on her lack of experience. She quickly created some wonderful, surreal paintings with the acrylics. Wasn't long before I convinced her to try her hand with oils.

When we went back to the art supply store for more supplies, canvases, and this time oils, we ran into a couple who were acquaintances of ours. They were older, retired. The woman had taken a liking to my wife and, as the two compared notes as to why they were both in the art supplies store, our acquaintance dropped that she was taking an art class once a week with other women in the community. As Divine Providence would have it, at that moment the teacher of the art class happened to walk into the same store! Our acquaintance introduced her to my wife and an instant friendship was formed. She invited my wife to the class. My wife accepted. The beautiful oil paintings on the walls of our dining room and salon attest to her talents and affinity for the class and painting.

I became her coach and critic. Early on, one of the things that I noticed was she would get so caught up in the details of a particular part

---

12 Another rule of trial work, one that will be repeated again and again in this book: "You can't win unless you believe you can." A lack of self-esteem, of self-confidence is probably the heart of every ill of the human condition. This defeatist attitude has no place in trial work. Cynical or, better yet, realistic, yes. Defeatist, never.

of the work that she forgot to step back to see how it fit into the painting as a whole. I realized I had to remind her: big picture (literally!). Every so often she needed to take a step back to see if the detail she was working on and developing actually complemented the rest of the painting. It's very common to get so caught up with a detail or theory and forget that it still needs to fit into, and complement, the whole. That can be hard. But what's even harder is to discard it if, it turns out, it doesn't fit. We become emotionally attached. But if the big picture can't be supported by the details (little picture) or the detail (little picture) doesn't fit into the theory of the case or prove an element (big picture), it may be time to discard it. I would encourage my wife, "Don't think that whatever Picasso or Monet you're admiring was the first attempt or even the first canvas! I'll guarantee more than one canvas made it into the trash before the picture hanging on the wall in the museum was considered a final product."

Every so often, step back. Take a look at how the details—the jury instructions, evidence (witness statements and interviews, photographs, videos, documents, etc.)—fit into your theory of the case, into your closing argument. If something doesn't fit, it's time to reassess that piece of evidence or your theory of the case.[13] Your closing argument, the outline of it, the thought of it is your guide throughout the entirety of litigation.

Know Your Elements/Know Your Facts and Be Flexible

Marissa spent her adolescent years and adult life trying to help people. A teenage karate champion, she taught and mentored kids and volunteered in her community. As a cadet with the Huntington Park Police Department, she'd volunteered to help in the Juveniles at Risk (JAR) bootcamp program. She'd grown up in the area and knew the challenges facing a lot of the kids

---

13 As a law clerk waiting for my bar results, I once asked the attorney I was clerking for what was one of his "secrets" to success at trial. He said that when he was just starting out, an older, wiser attorney told him, "Have your theory of the case, your 'script.' But don't be afraid to go off script. Learn how to roll with the evidence. You never know exactly what a witness is actually going to say until they say it. Attorneys that stick to a script always end up lost at some point during the trial." Getting an opposing attorney to go off script is a trial tactic that, when I am able, has served me well.

who would find themselves in that program. Volunteering to be a part of the program once she became a sworn police officer seemed natural.

Flash forward to the Leadership Empowerment and Development program (LEADS), the JAR program renamed. It was 2018, and this year the program/bootcamp had more applicants than in any previous years. Two local agencies, Huntington Park and a neighboring city, Southgate, assigned officers to act as the supervisors/caretakers/instructors for the program. A national guard base in scenic San Luis Obispo had become the annual setting for the weeklong bootcamp. About thirty boys and girls from Huntington Park and Southgate were enrolled by their parents to attend the camp.

Midway through the week, things went awry. Allegations of abuse and mismanagement made media headlines. About six officers were under investigation, including Marissa. A few weeks after the initial stories came out, Marissa, along with two other officers, was charged with abusing several kids.

Marissa was shocked, angry, hurt. Not only had she not abused anyone, but throughout the years, she'd poured her heart and soul into the program. Now, baseless allegations led to criminal charges, potentially ending a career that she'd worked so hard to achieve and landed her in custody as well.

Referred to me by some colleagues and friends, she called one night in tears. We talked for a while. I assured her I'd/we'd do everything we could to get her through it, G-d willing.

Partway through my workup of the case, I took on a younger, relatively new attorney in my firm, Nicole Pifari, to help with the workup but mostly to research and write some motions, and to train and mentor her in trial work.

After discussing the legal issues with Nicole at length, we both knew the biggest issue with the case was that our client was being tried with two other officers whose case presented much worse than ours. If we had any chance of winning, it would *not* be sitting next to the codefendants at trial. Guilt by association is a powerful handicap. Having to impeach teenage witnesses would present enough of a challenge. Having to also distance ourselves from the codefendants both by argument as well as perception would prove nearly impossible. Nicole researched and wrote a great severance motion to get us "severed" from the other two defendants. I told her that it was well researched, well written, and "should win in a perfect world." But in my twenty-five-plus years of practice (at the time), I simply didn't remember seeing a severance motion granted. Ever. She told me to have some faith! I laughed and told her I did, but it wasn't blind!

Well, turns out we had an intelligent, conscientious, and thoughtful judge who really understood our arguments and . . . *granted* the motion! Happy to eat my words, we could now roll up our sleeves without having two other defendants weighing down or negatively influencing our defense. Another pretrial motion allowed us to argue (because it was true) that Marissa was on duty at the time of the alleged incidents acting as a paid, sworn police officer. That would allow us to argue her training and experience in explaining her actions, or so we thought.

The trial went well. I impeached the first alleged victim (Jane Doe #1) on cross-examination by some prior inconsistent statements as well as her troubled, less-than-puritan background. It became obvious that she was either a pathological liar or, at the very least, someone who had a history of stretching the truth. She also had a history of violence—acting out, violent anxiety attacks, you name it. Her testimony, coupled with the second alleged victim's (Jane Doe #2) who testified on cross-exam that she was now doing wonderfully in school and at home *due to the program*, worked to effectively diffuse and deflate the prosecution's case.

In an attempt to rehabilitate their case, the prosecution called as their last witness the detective who had originally interviewed the second teenager, "Detective Smith." He testified Jane Doe #2 had told him that, at one point during the week of the bootcamp, she'd been placed in a utility closet as a punishment for an entire day and night and given only the barest amount of food and a wet blanket to sleep with, also for a punishment, for not following directions. He further testified that Jane Doe #2 claimed it was my client that had been in charge of her and had placed her in the closet, although she herself had not testified to that. Sounded like abuse. Sounded bad.

But it was false! Jane Doe #2 *never* said that. The detective was self-servingly testifying to his *very loose interpretation* of her statement. (And yes, I know we've been talking about the closing argument. But it's all tied together, so consider this a bonus/preview of some advice for cross-examination, which will tie into the closing argument at the end: *think outside the box.*)

The "standard" approach would have been to take out the transcript of the interview from my trial notebook, give a copy to the witness, and go through it, impeaching his "interpretation." And that usually works just fine. But I didn't want to just impeach the detective. *I wanted to implicate the prosecutors, too*, to have their credibility *and their case* called into question. So I didn't pull out my copies of Jane Doe #2's interview transcript. Instead, before I began that section of my cross-exam, I asked him for a verbatim of what Jane Doe #2 had said, which of course he couldn't remember. I asked him if reading the transcripts would refresh his memory, which of course he said it would. I then turned, in open court, in front of the jury, to the prosecutors and asked very innocently but firmly if "I could please borrow" *their* copy of the interview transcript to show the witness!

What could they say, no? In front of the jury?[14]

So, anxiously looking through their trial notebook, one of them pulled out the copy. I thanked them and then proceeded to go through it, pound for pound, each time refreshing his memory with a different page, a different line, walking back and forth to the witness stand on each occasion (I purposefully only had the prosecutor's copy), ending each "impeachment" series of questions with "and that was from the prosecutor's transcript that they had in their materials, the one they just gave me, right?" When the cross-examination was done, so was he and their case.

Or again, so we thought. One of the motions the judge held in abeyance was whether we could bring in our client's training and experience as a police officer to explain her actions, as well as a use of force expert. It was now time for our case-in-chief, and the judge ruled . . . *no*, on both! No evidence of training, experience, and no expert. And no jury instructions on those issues either. Marissa was devasted! The judge's rulings seemed to revive the prosecution's case just in time for closing arguments. I had to rework my closing arguments, the PowerPoint slides, even part of our theory of the case.

---

14 This is another example of knowing your judge. Our judge was very even-tempered, thoughtful, and disliked any confrontation. I assumed, correctly, she would not "butt into" my "antics" of asking to borrow their transcript rather than foraging for my own, if I asked innocently enough.

Let me explain. In police officer use of force cases, the seminal case outlining the standard to be used in analyzing the use of force is *Graham v. Connor*, 490 U.S. 386 (1989). In that case, plaintiff Graham, a diabetic suffering from a poor insulin reaction, was driven to a local store by a friend to buy a container of orange juice. When he found the line to be too long a wait, he ran back out. Connor, a police officer, thinking the quick entry and exit was suspicious and fearing a crime may have occurred, followed Graham and his friend and stopped the vehicle. He directed both to wait until he had backup officers and had time to investigate if, indeed, a crime had occurred. Graham tried to explain his condition to responding officers, to no avail. Fearing he was about to suffer a diabetic seizure, he resisted their attempts to detain him. In the ensuing confrontation, he sustained multiple injuries and sued the officers for excessive force.

In a unanimous decision, the Supreme Court held that all law enforcement uses of force must be analyzed under a Fourth Amendment/Search and Seizure "objective reasonableness" standard. One of the components of that analysis is whether the officers' actions are "objectively reasonable" in light of the facts confronting them, without regard to their underlying intent or motivation. The "reasonableness" of a particular use of force must be judged from the perspective of a reasonable officer on the scene . . . In other words, it is an objective analysis, and the officer's training and experience are relevant to that analysis.

Like in most police officer use of force cases, then, we had planned on making that objective analysis the heart of our argument, that Marissa was acting consistent with her training and experience and used reasonable force to overcome the resistance of Jane Doe #1. When police officers need to use force to overcome resistance, it's almost a given the person on the receiving end will think the contact is "offensive." So what? It's part of their job—police officer contact is *always* offensive to the person on the receiving end. No one likes being detained physically, let alone arrested. That was our argument from day one.

PowerPoint was done.

Closing argument was ready to go.

Until the judge's ruling.

That night I had to drive to Bakersfield, about two hours away, for an internal affairs interview of a different client. Maybe not the best idea the night before my closing argument, but in reality, it gave me time to think about reworking the closing. I spent the first half of the ride, on the way to Bakersfield, talking to G-d. Asking Him for help, for an idea, something to argue in place of the police officer training/use of force arguments. Most of the time when I'm in trial, I ask G-d that, if anything, please don't let me mess this up! I asked that, and more, on the way to Bakersfield.

One of my approaches for all my closing arguments is that, regardless of how prepared they are, I try to incorporate into the very beginning of each one some point the prosecutor just made, and then knock it down, as a way of setting the tone. In this case my client had, in fact, touched the first teenager, but not the way or for the reasons Jane Doe #1 testified. The teenager had been experiencing another anxiety attack after being placed in the back seat of a van for a "timeout" by another officer. When Marissa went to check on her, she was having a violent fit. Afraid she'd hurt herself, Marissa went into the van and put her hand on the girl's upper chest to both hold her down and calm her. It worked. The girl was now alleging a chokehold, but I felt we'd impeached that pretty well in cross-exam. Based on the elements for the child abuse counts, I thought we'd gotten enough out of Jane Doe #1 and #2 for our argument. Our fear was now, based on the legal definition of a battery (an "offensive" touching), Marissa could lose the lesser charge, and, if she did, she'd in effect lose everything: her ability to possess and carry a firearm, which meant her ability to remain a police officer. And being that the alleged victim was a teenager, it also meant jail. I needed not only a hook, but one sharp enough to deflate that element.

On the way back from Bakersfield, it happened. My hook. My introduction not only into that element, the "offensive" touching, but also *the entire* case. What started out as a seeming handicap, the judge's ruling became a gift. The judge had made me think outside the box. She'd done me a favor. I quicky called Nicole (who was back at the hotel in her room) and told her my thought process and began to dictate the new "opening" of my closing argument. The hook?

Don't Be Afraid to Challenge Your Jury

A lot of lawyers bend over backward to thank jurors at the beginning of their closing arguments, almost apologizing that they had to sit through the trial. Maybe it works for some. I think it sounds weak. We'll talk about that more in the section on voir dire. Over the years, I've learned to challenge my juries. Challenge them to be objective, to hold the prosecutor to their burden, the standard of proof. Challenge them to be fair. Challenge them to do their job, to honor their oath.

"*We trust you.*" Those three words, when together, can be the most powerful words in the English language (along with "I trust you," which I was trained to never use the word "I" in court unless specifically asked by the judge). When you challenge someone by challenging their sense of fairness, integrity, and *their loyalty to their sense of fairness and integrity*, which in a sense is what trust really is, you empower them. It ignites in them a desire to honor that trust and not betray it. It *connects you with them*. I talk about it often in voir dire. I like to begin and end with it in the closing argument.

Now, back to Marissa's case, the detective's less than forthright testimony, and the prosecution's seeming collusion with it. I began my argument that "the definition of what was 'offensive' wasn't really spelled out that well in the jury instructions" (in this case, the context was, admittedly, a touching, which wasn't quite my spin at that moment). Sure, the instructions referred to an unwanted touching, but obviously in life there are unwanted "touches" that are necessary. Are they crimes? Should they be? So far, so good. Then I turned the page on the Power-Point. The slide was simply the detective's name:

"Detective Smith."

Looking at the jury, I turned more serious, even a bit angry.

"What's offensive? This is what is offensive, folks. Detective Smith got on that stand and summarized and quoted Jane Doe #2's interview, and it was *not* what she'd said, *and . . .*" I turned and looked straight at both prosecutors, then pointed a finger, "*they knew that* because they had a transcript of what Jane Doe #2 said, word for word! *They* put Detective Smith on the stand, asked him questions, received answers that *they knew* were false, and said nothing! Never corrected him from *their* own transcript, not once! Is that honest? Is that right? Is that the kind of evidence, the kind of trial you'd expect from the ones who claim to be seeking justice? *That's offensive!*" I almost shouted, my voice firm, holding back emotion.

"*That* should insult your intelligence! *That* should insult your sense of right and wrong! As we go through the evidence and the law together, now, in these next few minutes, let's not forget about Detective Smith. As we walk through the elements the prosecution has to prove, like an 'offensive' touching, ask yourself what's **really offensive**: Officer Larios' touching, to help calm and, in the end, protect a troubled teenager exhibiting a violent anxiety attack, or the offensive way this case has been tried, and argued, by the government. We picked you to be fair. We picked you because *we trust you*. We *trust* you can be objective. We *trust* you can hold the government to their burden of proof. We *trust you* can be honest about the evidence. That you aren't just a rubber stamp but instead, twelve intelligent, impartial, fair-minded people who can see this case, and how the government has tried it, for what it is.

"*We trust you.* This case should insult your intelligence."

We won the case. Not guilty across the board.

Know your facts. Challenge the jury. Be flexible. Think outside the box. I didn't have to find and thumb through notes or the actual transcript to know that Detective Smith's testimony was self-servingly off. I had read and listened to that interview so many times that I had basically memorized it, word for word. Knowing that interview cold allowed me to jump right into cross-exam without a pause and, when the time came, to use *their* transcript, without my highlights, without my notes, again without a pause.

Their transcript, with all its implications. Seamless.

A trial is as much a morality play as it is a legal proceeding. Juries like to think they're erring on the side of what's "right." Presentation, preparedness, assuredness, and being able to take the "high road" are factors never to be underestimated. I've found that most people, by nature, think that if it's the truth or if it's right, it doesn't need much preparation, which is completely wrong in trial work (we'll talk about preparation more in the next chapter). The more prepared you are and come across, the more honest you look and therefore the more believable you are. The more you *know* your facts and the elements/issues, the more equipped you are for those curve balls that will inevitably come your way. The more prepared for any scenario, the more convincing you will be. PowerPoints are great, but they're also crutches. They can be boring.

Know your facts.

Don't be afraid. Challenge your jury.

Structure

Although I'll weave into the other chapters more thoughts and advice on the closing argument, before we leave the chapter exclusively devoted to it, I thought it'd be good to talk a little about structure.

Either you already have or will develop your own style. That style will determine the structure of your closing arguments. One piece of advice that has helped me: Utilize pretty much the same structure each time. Sure, it may vary here and there depending on the type of case and the facts.

But in general, you should get used to structuring your closing arguments in a format that works for you and is consistent. Facts, the law, opponents, jurisdictions—obviously each trial has new variables to deal with. If the structure of your argument is always changing, too, then not only are you reinventing the wheel each time, which takes time and effort, but you're less grounded as well.

Remember, we start preparing from the beginning by at least outlining our closing arguments. The more familiar you are with your structure, the easier it will be to fit in the elements from the jury in-structions and your facts, and start forming your arguments. It'll flow in your mind and then to your paper (or PowerPoint).

A structure that has worked for me over the years, and remains flexible enough to incorporate facts from the trial that you didn't plan for, even (as I alluded to earlier) parts of the opposing counsel's argument, is as follows:

Your Introduction. Start with something not only important, but a "hook," like I described in the bootcamp case. It could be a fact or argument that will act as a theme throughout your whole presentation, for example, a story[15] or analogy directly related to the case. Make it something that grabs the jury or judge. Sometimes labeling something the key fact, the key piece of testimony, and hitting on it not in full but

---

15 We'll talk more about the use of stories later on in the book.

enough to make your point, leaves the listener "wanting more." Now they're paying attention; you can then segue into how this fact or element should be interpreted and analyzed.

The Standard of Proof/Burden of Proof. How should the jury approach the weighing of the evidence, the determination of the facts? In trial work, we're asking jurors to use a system, an approach to problem-solving that is completely foreign to them. In everyday life, no one has the time or patience to weigh each fact and facet of a situation before making a decision about what is acceptable and what is not. Moreover, the rules of evidence—like hearsay and its multitude of exceptions, laying a proper foundation for the evidence, relevance, a fact being deemed more prejudicial to one side than probative, and a referee of sorts (a judge) deciding these things—simply don't exist in our daily lives. Finally, in everyday life there's no legal standard mandating, based on what we do know and are able to understand, how we decide which side to agree with. Would you win your argument with your wife or husband if you had to prove your point to her or him by proof beyond a reasonable doubt?! What if we lowered the standard to a preponderance of the evidence? And, as described above, what "evidence" would you be allowed to use in making your point?

Beginning my closing by acknowledging the forum and parameters within which the jury needs to work, and the foreign nature of that forum, again, connects me to them. I feel their "pain," meaning, I can relate. I'm empathizing with them. Usually, they appreciate it. It gives me credibility. So, when I tell them how to approach the legal standard at work, basically, how to do their job, they listen. I can then tie that to the jury instructions, the elements. All are interwoven pieces of one "tapestry," and now, their approach.[16]

---

16 There are general jury instructions that can be, and often are, more than helpful to go over and weave into your closing argument more than once. Being a criminal defense attorney in California, my personal favorite is what we call colloquially "The Circumstantial Evidence Instruction." I think it outlines not only the approach juries should take to weighing the evidence and applying the law, but it also defines a real, working definition for the prosecution's burden of proving each element beyond a reasonable doubt. When at all possible, I try to refer to it multiple times during closing argument. It is that powerful.

Evidence. Once I've "hooked" them, talked about the standard of proof at work and how to apply it by using the jury instructions, I then go into detail about the evidence but always, every so often, loop back to remind them of the standard of proof and how to marry the two together. I remind them to keep their eyes on the proverbial ball, to never lose sight of the forum we're in and the approach to take when going over the evidence. I've found the best way to do this, again, is with jury instructions. They're your guide, your consistent thread throughout that tapestry you're hopefully weaving.

If I have a difficult fact, a "bad" witness, I like to address it and deflate it in the beginning. Remember, I've already "hooked" them in the opening to my argument. I've built credibility; I've acknowledged the forum and approach they have to utilize in order to problem-solve. As stated in the bootcamp case, I've told them that we trust them. With all of that, I have the standing, authority, and credibility to take on a bad fact and get rid of it, or at least deflate it. Once done, I can move on to evidence that helps my case, strengthens my arguments while again weaving in the jury instructions, the elements.

Jury Instructions. Jury instructions, the law the jury will be utilizing in deciding the case, are the frame and foundation of the proverbial house you've built during the trial. As I stated at the beginning of the chapter, the first thing I do in my trial preparation is pull the jury instructions that apply to the case. In structuring and drafting your closing argument, where and when you discuss those instructions in relation to the evidence, how to apply them to the evidence and how often, are decisions that can make or break your closing.

Which instructions you focus on can also make or break your presentation. Case in point: Probably the most useful, applicable, and most underestimated instruction in criminal cases in California is the California Criminal (CALCRIM) Instruction 224—the circumstantial evidence instruction. It's given whenever there is circumstantial evidence in a criminal trial. But...

The logic and principle behind and within the instruction, in reality, presents probably the best working definition of how to approach the evidence when the burden is proof beyond a reasonable doubt. Meaning: Even if your case is completely a direct evidence case, you can still utilize the underlying logic in this instruction in helping the jury understand their task within the system—to hold the prosecution to its burden of proof. And, obviously, even more so in a case with circumstantial evidence. Let's look at the instruction and then "apply" the logic, in a general way.

> CALCRIM 224 reads as follows:
> 224. Circumstantial Evidence: Sufficiency of Evidence
> "Before you may rely on circumstantial evidence to conclude that a fact necessary to find the defendant guilty has been proved, you must be convinced that the People have proved each fact essential to that conclusion beyond a reasonable doubt. Also, before you may rely on circumstantial evidence to find the defendant guilty, you must be convinced that the only reasonable conclusion supported by the circumstantial evidence is that the defendant is guilty. If you can draw two or more reasonable conclusions from the circumstantial evidence, and one of those reasonable conclusions points to innocence and another to guilt, you must accept the one that points to innocence. However, when considering circumstantial evidence, you must accept only reasonable conclusions and reject any that are unreasonable."

The instruction *mandates* that if there is more than one reasonable interpretation of the evidence, and one of those reasonable interpretations points to innocence, the jury *must* accept that interpretation and reject the other. Let's say that again. The jury must accept the interpretation that points to innocence. Which means it doesn't matter if the prosecution's argument or case makes sense or sounds reasonable. All that really matters is that there's another interpretation that points to innocence that also makes sense. And not even more sense. As long as it makes sense (i.e., is reasonable and points to innocence), it doesn't have to make more sense or be more reasonable. There is no comparing and contrasting here. If the defense interpretation is reasonable, we're done—game over! When arguing the interpretation or significance of a piece or pieces of evidence, this instruction is probably the most powerful tool in a defense attorney's arsenal.

But wait, there's more . . .

Taking the logic to its natural conclusion, what the instruction *really means* is that the prosecution's case not only needs to be reasonable, it needs to be so reasonable that it excludes any other reasonable inter-pretation or argument pointing toward innocence!

Did you see *that*?!

I'll write it again: The prosecution's case needs to be reasonable to the exclusion of any other reasonable interpretation or argument pointing toward innocence! And you can look the jury in the face and say, with all honesty and confidence, "That's the law!"

It makes sense too. Because if there really is another reasonable argument that points to innocence, shouldn't the defendant then get the benefit of that reasonable doubt? Isn't that what the burden of proof really means?

Isn't that what's really fair?

In the bootcamp case, although most of the evidence in the case was testimonial, there was some circumstantial evidence, so I got the instruction and utilized it to not only when speaking about that circum-stantial evidence but also to "instruct" the jury how to approach this foreign way of decision-making: holding the prosecution to meeting its burden beyond a *reasonable* doubt. I used the instruction's "logic" to argue that Marissa firmly putting her hand on the upper chest of Jane Doe #1 to calm her and keep her from hurting herself was a reasonable interpretation of the evidence and therefore the jury must adopt it.

Now you also have a hint how to "argue" that instruction even when you don't have circumstantial evidence in your case (And how much more so if you do!). Just use the logic to argue how the jury should approach reasonable doubt. Again, it makes common sense. It makes moral sense, even legal sense. And since the actual reason-able doubt instruction doesn't give any concrete method to determine a reasonable doubt and apply it, you have some latitude here. Many attorneys look closely at those instructions that define the elements in the case at hand, but they ignore the "usual" instructions, the general ones.

Don't.

Those instructions, like the example above, flesh out the specific cause of action instructions, and often help you deal with specific pieces of evidence or testimony or help the jury better understand how to apply the specific cause of action instructions.

Before we leave the subject of jury instructions (for now), let me make one more point. Although there is usually a specific instruction or set of instructions for the cause of action you're litigating, how those instructions apply to your case, and how they can (or cannot) be argued, may need to be researched in the case law. For example, CALCRIM 520 describing the elements for second-degree murder, implied malice states:

The defendant had *implied malice* if:

1. (He/She) intentionally (committed the act/[or] failed to act).
2. The natural and probable consequences of the (act/[or] failure to act) were dangerous to human life.
3. At the time (he/she) (acted/[or] failed to act), (he/she) knew (his/her) (act/[or] failure to act) was dangerous to human life.
and
4. (He/She) deliberately (acted/[or] failed to act) with conscious disregard for (human/[or] fetal) life.

Although the CALCRIM 520 speaks to the elements of implied malice, what does conscious disregard for human life mean? The case law speaks to "it is implied when no considerable provocation appears, or when the circumstances attending the killing show an abandoned and malignant heart" (California Penal Code section 188, cited in *People v. Blakely* (2000) 23 Cal.4th 500).

That language, especially what seems to be a caveat ("no considerable provocation") helps to better define implied malice in more practical terms.[17] Good language in the case law may allow you to request a special

---

17 As an aside to better expand on the above, voluntary manslaughter is a lesser offense to second degree murder. Depending on the specific facts of your case, if there is evidence that can be argued that at the moment your client committed the act that led to a death, he was reacting to what he felt was a considerable provocation on the part of the decedent, even though the act committed by your client foreseeably could result in death, he may not be guilty of second-degree murder. What's the next step in the analysis? A considerable provocation really means that the decedent did something that caused your client to be in fear for his life. If your client's fear, based on that considerable provocation, was reasonable, he's not guilty of second-degree murder. If it was unreasonable, which really means that objectively the provocation was not considerable, but his fear was sincere, meaning honest, he may be guilty of manslaughter.

instruction, further explaining that somewhat vague and ambiguous phrase, or at least by factual analogy see how you might argue it.[18]

Stories. There was a Hasidic sage, Michel of Vitebsk, who once said, "G-d created people because He loves stories." People ARE stories, each person a story unto themselves. Our own personal novels are constantly being written. That being the case, it's been my experience that juries love stories, too, or at least analogies. A good analogy from everyday life makes the foreignness of the forum palatable and less intimidating. And it drives home the point more powerfully than an overt argument.

One "story" I've used countless times is the bowl of cereal story. When arguing that the prosecution case has discrepancies and/or problems, or that witnesses have either contradicted themselves within their own testimonies, or other pieces of evidence, this story works like a charm.

Picture this:

It's early Sunday morning. My son Joey, who's about eight years old, comes into the kitchen, still rubbing some sleep from his eyes. He walks over to the cabinet, takes out a box of Frosted Flakes (with Tony the Tiger on the front—we'll talk more about that in the chapter on voir dire), and pours himself a bowl. Add a spoon and some milk, and voila!

Breakfast.

Here's where I come in, and the jury too.

Walking into the kitchen, I see Joey get up from the table and walk over to the garbage, about to empty the full bowl of cereal into the trash. "Joey, what're you doing?" I ask firm enough to stop the waste of food.

"There was a bug in the cereal," he replies.

"So you're going to waste an entire bowl of cereal for one bug?" I respond, walking toward him. I take his spoon, swipe up the bug, making sure there's some milk "buffer" around the floating insect, and dump the spoon's contents into the garbage. I rinse off the spoon in the sink to eliminate any bug "contamination" and hand the spoon back to Joey.

"Here, no more bug," I smile.

---

18 One of the best places to start researching your jury instructions is the bench notes, outlined after the body of the instruction. Updated instructions should have updated case law, but like any other research, the cases in the bench notes should always be shepardized.

"Aba, I'm not going to eat that, there was a bug in it."

"Joey, I took it out. It's gone. You're not wasting a whole bowl of cereal. Go sit and eat."

Begrudgingly, he walks back to the table, puts down the bowl, picks up his spoon. Satisfied that I'd "won," I turn and begin to walk away.

"Aba," stops me in my tracks. "I found another bug."

Turning, I walk back to the table and look down. Another bug. I take the spoon, and same routine: scoop out the bug with the milk buffer around it, dump it into the trash, rinse off the spoon, and hand it back.

"I'm not eating this. It had two bugs!" Joey says more firmly and a bit more disgusted.

"Joey, they're gone. It's fine." I turn around. I'm losing patience, but I'm also losing my resolve. Then . . .

"Aba, I found another bug. I'm *not* eating this!"

I look at the jury. Some of them are smirking. They can relate.

"How many bugs does your son have to find in a bowl of cereal before you stop making the poor kid eat it, and throw it out?"

Leaning in, almost to create a more private conversation, I'll continue.

"And if there's that many bugs in the bowl, what about the box? Probably infested. You think Joey, or anyone else in the house he tells about the bugs in the bowl, will touch that box of Frosted Flakes? Might as well throw out the box. Is it worth the headache of fighting with your kid? Or making him eat a bowl of cereal after he finds bug after bug? After all, it's only a $2.50 box of cereal."

I lean in more. "What about a man's life, his reputation, his freedom? How many bugs do you have to find in the prosecutor's case before you throw out the box?!"

"We don't keep an infested box of cereal that only costs two or three dollars. A person's liberty? Their freedom? Why would you let the prosecutor force you to swallow so-and-so's testimony?" Then back to the burden of proof, perhaps the jury instruction on conflicting testimony.

Stories and/or everyday analogies. Real life is always vivid and very powerful.

Conclusion. You've gone through your argument, the evidence, the jury instructions, maybe a story, and now you need to bring it home. Connecting to the beginning is a nice way of bringing things full circle.

Pick a powerful point from the beginning of your argument or maybe an example or analogy, even from voir dire, and weave it into your conclusion. Wind your way to the standard of proof or the best instruction for your case. These are now all reminders, so they are quick.

You can now wax poetic too. It's the end. I like to end with a story that illustrates the whole case, or one of the major issues in the case, and then, finally, again:

We're trusting you.

Challenge the jury to not betray your trust. To not betray their sense of fairness or justice. It was mentioned in voir dire, in the opening statement, at the beginning of your closing, and now at the end. Full circle. Over time, you'll develop what works for you. I trust you (wink).

CLOSING ARGUMENT
Compass Points

• • •

A. Know Your Elements–Jury Instructions

- Look up the law that outlines the elements you need to prove or defend against.
- Start to formulate how your facts fit into the law/legal principles governing your case.
- Go over the evidence as you know it at the time:

  ✓ *What evidence do you have right now that fits into your theory of the case?*

  ✓ *What evidence do you still need, if any, to strengthen or prove your case?*

  ✓ *What evidence do you need, if any, to rebut the other side's case?*

- How would you then weave that evidence into your theory of the case?

  ✓ *Your theory of the case should be able to resonate with your audience: the morality play.*

B. Big picture/little picture

- Look at big points first.

  ✓ *Big points mean big picture.*

  ✓ *Elements are big picture.*

  ✓ *Theory of the case is big picture.*

  ✓ *Narrative is big picture.*

- Little picture second.

  ✓ *The evidence is little picture.*

  ✓ *Constant exercise—how does your evidence (little picture) fit into the big picture?*

- Know your evidence/know your facts—COLD!
- Be flexible—be able to go off script.

C. Structure
- Introduction—A hook
  - ✓ *Challenge your jury.*
  - ✓ *"We trust you."*
- Standard of proof/burden of proof
  - ✓ *Jury Instructions*
  - ✓ *Principles spoken about in voir dire*
- Evidence
  - ✓ *Address "bad" facts in the beginning, after your hook, to deflate them right away and get to your strengths.*
  - ✓ *Strong fact(s)/evidence*
  - ✓ *Jury Instructions*
  - ✓ *Strength over chronological order (if it's easy to follow)*

D. Stories

E. Conclusion—bring it home full circle.

CHAPTER THREE

PREPARATION

Give me six hours to chop down a tree and I will spend the first four sharpening the axe.

—ABRAHAM LINCOLN

A trial is a living, breathing entity. It has an energy. You can feel it, and once felt, you can tap into it and influence it. Too many attorneys are spectators in their own litigation. For them, if it's not in their script, it doesn't exist. But living things don't follow a script, at least not completely. And neither do trials.

Be flexible. In your trial preparation and in your execution in court. Have a theme or theory of your case, yes. But have not only a plan A, but also a plan B and plan C for those pieces of evidence that may not come out as planned, or those legal curveballs the judge may throw you before or during trial.

For anyone who has ever played in or has been a fan of a competitive sport, the idea that a trial has a life and energy of its own is not foreign. Like in a game or match, you can feel it. Momentum, and the shift of momentum. Highs. Lows. Just like sporting events, trials are alive. The more you contribute to the energy, take control of certain parts, the more you influence it and connect to it.

Like the old commercial that said, "Never let them see you sweat." Self-confidence is a primary way of connecting to and, therefore, influencing that dynamic.

Houdini and the Elderly Nurse

A lost battle is a battle one thinks one has lost.
—JEAN-PAUL SARTRE

One Friday night at our Shabbos (Sabbath) table, my daughter told a story she'd heard in school.

Back some time in the early part of the twentieth century, Harry Houdini was a household name. A master magician and escape artist, it seemed there wasn't any physical challenge he couldn't overcome. People traveled miles just to catch a glimpse of the mysterious man and his next impossible escape. But for Harry Houdini, it was the heroic feats of a grandmother that challenged his hold on reality to such an extent that he traveled halfway across the country just to meet *her*!

The grandmother had been in her home when she heard what sounded like a car crash in front of her house. Knowing her grandson was outside playing, she quickly stopped what she was doing and ran out the front door only to see her grandson in the middle of the street, pinned under a car. Being a registered nurse for most of her adult life, she quickly gleaned from what she could see that if the car either backed up or rolled forward, based on her grandson's precarious position, his head would be crushed.

They lived in a semi-rural area. No help would be there for some time. If she waited that long, her grandson might die just from the weight of the car on him. She felt helpless. All of these feelings, she'd later relate, raced through her mind in probably less than a second.

But a second was more than she could stand. She ran down her porch as fast as she could to the car, and with Herculean strength, lifted the car off her grandson. The driver, already out of the car and at a loss himself of what to do, in shock at what he'd just witnessed, grabbed the boy and pulled him to safety. The youngster fully recovered.

Back in the day of no internet, no social media, and no "Google" search, the story still made headlines across the country. But what was even more curious was the fact that the elderly nurse refused to discuss with anyone what she was thinking before and during her miraculous rescue of her grandson. Reporter after reporter, and attempted interview after attempted interview bore no fruit.

Houdini was mesmerized by the story. An international celebrity at the time, his trip to visit the woman, by itself, became news. Reporters' cameras flashed at the couple sitting in her living room; pens were poised, assuming that with such a famous, popular figure making the trek just for her, she'd talk.

She didn't. Even for Houdini, she refused to say what she was thinking before and during her rescue of her grandson.

Houdini got up to leave. He asked the cameramen to leave the house, the reporters to wait outside. Then he smiled.

"They're all gone," he quietly reassured her. "Even if you don't want to tell me what you were thinking, can you at least tell me why you won't say it?"

Maybe it was Houdini's innate charisma. Maybe it was the woman's need to finally confide in someone. She stared at the celebrity for a minute. Then with her hand, the elderly woman motioned for him to sit back down.

"When I was a young woman, I dreamed of becoming a doctor. It was all that I wanted since I could even say the word. I played doctor with friends; I asked our family doctor so many questions he sometimes refused to let me in his office!

"I worked hard in school, real hard. I got great grades. I knew that a woman becoming a doctor, especially in those days, at the beginning of the century, was rare to none. But I'd be different. I'd show everyone.

"I got into college, and again, worked hard. I got all As, too. When I was a junior, I applied to medical school. Rejection letter after rejection letter chipped away at my dream, my resolve. When I finally got accepted to one, I thought that was it! Now all I had to do was work hard again and I'd realize my dream.

"Medical school for a woman, the only one at the time in my first-year class, was hell. I was laughed at, sneered at, ignored, touched, belittled, even spat at. My self-esteem, self-confidence, my resolve finally broke.

"I quit.

"I went into nursing. Women weren't doctors, I'd been told. Women were nurses. I resigned myself that that was my reality. For thirty years, I was a nurse. I put my dream of being a doctor in a box, locked it, and threw away the key.

"Until the day my grandson got run over by the car. What was I thinking when I heard the tires screech? When I ran outside to him stuck under the car, slowly being crushed? I really can't tell you what I thought in that moment. I can't. To this day, I haven't told anyone. But I can tell you *why* I won't.

"After I saved him, after the camera lights stopped flashing, it hit me. If I had the power, the resolve, the strength to lift a car off my grandson, then I'd had the strength to stay in medical school and suffer all the humiliation and challenges and become a doctor! Why did I quit?! I kept beating myself up. I could've done it! I could've been a doctor!

"The thought of it, all of it, even my saving my grandson, became too painful." She began to cry. "Of course, I'm thankful to G-d for saving my grandson. But if I could believe in myself then, why couldn't I believe in myself back then?" Wiping away his own tear, Houdini understood. He got up, wished her all the best, and began to walk out the front door where his car and the myriad of press was still waiting. They all asked him if she had confided in him what she'd told no one else. He shook his head and smiled, but he said nothing. Somewhere in his head, in his soul he could hear her whispering, still, from inside her house, "*I could've been a doctor. I could've been a doctor.*"

We can't succeed unless we believe we can. It's a lesson for trials, and a lesson for life.

In his book, *Think and Grow Rich*, Napoleon Hill delineates six steps for success. According to Hill, one of the most crucial steps is "faith." He directs the reader to outline a formula in the form of a mantra, describing what steps/work/effort (he describes it as sacrifices) the person is willing to take, with a specific goal and a specific deadline to meet that goal. He then states that the reader should repeat the mantra out loud at least twice a day, once upon waking and once when going to bed. He also strongly suggests the reader think about and state out loud the mantra at other times during the day and never allow a day to go by without working toward that goal.

Ironically, when I read his book, I realized that at least in my trial work, I had already incorporated part of his formula into my practice. When getting a new case that I feel will most likely go to trial, I think about it constantly, on and off, day in and day out. Some days, I spent tangibly working on the case; some days, I spent just dwelling on it. I also have a habit of visualizing and "hearing" the clerk reading aloud the verdict. All the time. Every day: "We, the jury, in the above entitled action find the defendant, [Joe Schmo], not guilty of a violation of penal code [such and such] . . ."[19] Once I'm actually in trial, it's a constant; I'm able to then visualize the courtroom clerk in my trial court saying it.

Hill's focus on faith (he capitalizes it) is a recognition that we're not really in control, that we need to attach ourselves to a higher, greater reality.[20] And he advises the reader that one of the steps in doing that is to verbalize the outcome or goal you want. As a person of faith, for me the higher intelligence is G-d. A student of Carl Jung would call it the universal consciousness. Luke Skywalker would call it the Force. Call it what you like. I don't know the master plan, but recognizing there is one and trying to influence its outcome by attaching yourself to it puts your case, you, your life, into a greater context. Verbalizing that goal can, and has for me (and Hill, for that matter), made that goal a reality.[21] I also verbalize phrases and thoughts from cross-examinations, closing arguments, even voir dire—sometimes to myself, sometimes in conversations with colleagues, clients, and family.

---

19 In the context of the book, Hill focuses on wealth but does qualify it, if only between the lines, to outline steps to achieve whatever goal a person is striving for. One is verbalizing that goal. For more on this concept, it's highly recommended to read the book, *Think and Grow Rich* by Napoleon Hill (Ballantine Books, 1937, renewed 1988).

20 Hill calls it the "Higher Intelligence."

21 As a side note, on cases where I can't seem to verbalize the verdict with confidence, I've not seen a solidly positive outcome. Some have resulted in hung juries, some convictions. Spooky?

It works. You can't win unless you think you can, unless you know you can.[22]

In January of 2001, I left being a public defender for what I thought were greener pastures: the private sector. While working as a senior felony attorney in the Riverside County public defender's office, I was offered a job by the senior partner of the law firm our fledgling union had used to help us to form our own bargaining group. The firm's niche was defending public employees, specifically police officers and firefighters. They had a partner who was the only lawyer in the office handling criminal matters and felt that they needed a second attorney with criminal defense experience to help him with his case load.

It was ten years after the Rodney King case and the reality was that cops were beginning to get into trouble more often. The job meant more money, more autonomy, and an office much closer to home. I was about to get married, and my home base would be Los Angeles, an hour and a half drive from Riverside. The police defense firm's office was in Santa Monica. It seemed more than providential.

Five years after taking the job, things weren't exactly working to perfection. I'd had only one criminal trial in those five years, a far cry from my average of nearly eight to ten a year in Riverside, and even more in Ventura. The political climate in the office was less than pleasant as well. All were good people, but good people don't always get along. The police unions billed very low hourly rates, so the way to make any money was to grind out long hours. I had a new family. In 2006, my three kids were four, two, and one years old. Housing prices

---

22 We have all overcome challenges in our lives. Even getting through daily work-outs can be counted as small accomplishments. When I was in first and second grade, I had a speech impediment. I couldn't pronounce my "s" and "sh," my "l" came from the back of my throat, and I confused my "m" with an "n." For two years, twice a week, I was pulled out of class for an hour of speech therapy. It was embarrassing. At home, I had practice worksheets. It was only about fifteen minutes a night, but for those fifteen minutes I put my mother and father through purgatory. My parents, however, were not discouraged; they sat with me, night after night, until I got it right. When I complained, my father would say "You're going to do this. *You never know, maybe you'll grow up to be a public speaker one day and need to be able to articulate properly.*"

had skyrocketed. Being an orthodox Jew, at least two of my kids were now in private religious schools (one in kindergarten, one in pre-nursery). Rents had increased as well.

My salary hadn't. My hours, although more than admirable in government work, were not high enough for my firm to give me a raise. The carrot they were holding out for another 200–300 more billable hours, which meant giving up that family time with my wife and small children, to be blunt, felt like crumbs given how many hours more I'd have to bill to get it. Maybe it was all they felt they could afford. After all, the unions' hourlies were extremely low. But it wasn't enough to make even a dent in my budget woes. I was in a state of constant defensiveness at work, and financial anxiety (with all the other stresses that brings) at home.

Then I met Ivory Webb.

It was Rosh Chodesh Shevat, the first day of the Jewish month of Shevat on the Jewish calendar. I was on call, meaning that if an officer member in one of the unions we represented was in an officer-involved shooting (OIS) or a critical incident like a death in custody, I was the attorney on call to drive to the officer's location. (Usually, by the time we got the call, the officer had already been taken from the scene and transported to his or her station or a hospital if they were hurt.) We'd hear them out regarding what happened, spot issues (if there were any), help them jog their memory or simply articulate their experience better. We'd also advise them of all the liabilities they were now facing, the foremost being criminal liability if the shooting or death was found to be unjustified by either the county district attorney's office or the US attorney's office (who at this time rarely looked at this stuff). Bottom line: They were now suspects in a potential crime. If the suspect they shot was dead, and the shooting was determined to be unjustified, they could be charged with murder. If he was still alive, the officer could be charged with assault with a deadly weapon, assault under color of authority, or even attempted murder. We'd help them decide if they should give a voluntary interview to criminal investigators, given all the circumstances and above considerations.

I remember seeing my cell phone light up. It was on silent—I was in the middle of my morning prayers in synagogue. Prayers were longer that day, too, given that it was a special day on the Jewish calendar. I looked at my prayer book and then, again, back down at my phone. Still blinking. I picked up the phone, discreetly walked out the back, and answered.

It was an OIS involving a San Bernardino deputy sheriff. His name was Ivory Webb. The case would become national, in fact international, news. It would be the case that eventually catapulted my career. But back then, I didn't know that. Broke, working at a firm that was becoming more stressful by the moment, a wife and three small children to support, all I knew was that I'd have to now wrap up my prayers as fast as I could (including, literally, wrapping up my phylacteries, prayer shawl, and prayer book) and drive the hour and a half to the Chino Hills station to meet the deputy.

Chino Hills is an affluent city in the southwestern part of San Bernardino County that contracted out their police department to the sheriff's department. At the time, Ivory Webb was a patrol deputy assigned to that station. It was his Friday. He was due to go on vacation for two weeks the very next day.

G-d had another plan. That night, unbeknownst to Ivory or his partners, an airman home on leave from the Air Force had decided to throw himself a barbecue party at his parents' house in Montclair, one city next to Chino Hills. Although he had made good, leaving his neighborhood and some ne'er-do-well friends to join the Air Force, he invited those same friends to the barbecue. They got drunk, as old high-school friends do, and at one point one of them borrowed a Corvette from another partygoer and asked the airman if he'd like to go for a ride. After blowing one or two stop signs, an on-duty deputy tried to pull them over. They didn't comply and the ensuing pursuit would travel through an industrial complex to a residential area, all the while the drunken friends were blowing past stop signs, red lights, you name it, and at times reaching speeds of over a hundred miles an hour. The deputy soon lost the Corvette.

Ivory heard the chase and staged on a side street, hoping to fall in behind his partner. What he didn't plan for was the chase coming right to him. He was talking to his wife on the phone, monitoring his partner's pursuit when the Corvette made a hard right onto the street he'd been staging on and drove directly at him. Ivory maneuvered to avoid a collision.

The car kept going. Ivory made a U-turn, trying to catch up. The Corvette made another hard right, tried a quick U-turn, lost control, and crashed into a brick wall on a dark street. Ivory came to a stop across the street, slightly ahead of where they'd crashed. The passenger tried getting out of the car. Ivory exited his patrol vehicle and ordered him to get on the ground. He didn't comply. He kept raising a hand, talking, challenging. The driver was yelling from inside the car, too, also challenging Ivory who, now by himself, was holding them both at gunpoint. Ivory had no idea where he was; they'd driven into Chino by this point. A standoff ensued. After a couple of minutes of challenges, orders, and noncompliance, Ivory seemed to tell the passenger, the on-leave airman, to get up. He was scared out of his mind, alone against what he thought at the time were two violent felony suspects. To this day, he doesn't remember saying it. But we all heard it.

"OK, get up . . . get up."

The passenger seemed to reach into his sweatshirt, then sprang up to all fours as if starting a race in Ivory's direction. Deputy Ivory Webb shot three times to stop what he sincerely thought was a threat to his life. The airman was hit with all three shots. He survived.

The entire standoff, including the shooting, was caught on video by a neighbor with a high-quality video camera. He showed the video to a shocked San Bernardino Sheriff's Department homicide unit that night. He also sold it to the media.

By the time I'd rolled up to Chino Hills station at eight thirty the next morning, Ivory had been sitting by himself in a small office for nearly eight hours. He didn't know he could call for legal representation. He didn't know he could have a lawyer. At 7:00 a.m. his captain came into the station, saw Ivory in the office, and asked him if he'd spoken to his attorney yet.

Ivory asked, "What attorney?"

The captain quickly called the union, who called me. I became that attorney.

The video had gone viral by the time I walked into the small room where Ivory was sitting. It was the first videotaped officer-involved shooting in the country to go viral contemporaneous to its occurrence. My parents in Florida saw it that morning. A behavioral psychologist we eventually called for trial, while training police officers in England, saw it that morning. It was everywhere.

A month later, Ivory Webb became the first San Bernardino law enforcement officer in nearly fifty years to be charged with a crime for an on-duty shooting.

Influences In and Out of Court

Believe it or not, lawyers are people too. And that means we can be influenced by all kinds of things, both professionally and personally. Those influences can severely impact our workup of a case, its execution in court, and our performance. Trial attorneys, even seasoned ones, need to be aware of this. I know some experienced trial lawyers who nearly quarantine themselves a month before trial. If that works, great. It's obviously not for everyone.

I try to stay the family man as much as possible because my family and religious/community life is the heart and soul (pun intended) of my existence, my sanity. I take long walks, and I exercise "religiously." And I try to stay very aware of my need to focus when I need to focus.

Bottom line: Besides living and breathing your trial, you need to keep in mind and keep in your routine those positive parts of your life that relieve stress and help you focus. You also need to keep out any negative influences that can add to the stress of a trial, which is already stressful.[23]

Ivory was a good man. Standing over 6 feet tall and weighing over 230 pounds, a college football star at the University of Iowa, he'd worked a few different sales jobs after college, but nothing clicked. His father was a retired chief from the Compton Police Department. The retail jobs having not worked out, it seemed natural for Ivory to enroll in a police academy; he picked the San Bernardino Sheriff's Department academy. Six months later, he was sworn in as a deputy sheriff.

Soft-spoken, pleasant, and intelligent, he soon became very well liked in the department. Fast-forward about ten years later, he was in line for the

---

23 Ivory's case, being in the Los Angeles Times almost weekly as well as the local San Bernardino/Inland Empire paper The Press-Enterprise, was already stressful. Add to that the pressure at the office, my financial situation, and the natural desire to win or at least do well for my client, and the stress at times felt overwhelming.

Public Information Officer (PIO) position: the deputy in charge of being the sheriff's spokesperson for the media. His star was beginning to rise.

The shooting ended all of that.

My career at the time was as tenuous as Ivory's future. In the small police defense niche, I was a nobody. Ivory's father, the retired chief of police, had heard of my boss, Bill, the senior partner, and wanted him to take over Ivory's defense. Bill was confident, personable, a highly skilled litigator, and an established name in the niche, even somewhat flamboyant at our first meeting with Ivory and his family. The contrast between the senior partner and me—an unknown, soft-spoken, religious guy from New York—was striking. Mr. Webb's concern was understandable. After all, this was his son's life. I had much more actual trial experience than Bill, more than most attorneys. But he was a known quantity in this niche, a name. I wasn't. My reserved style only added to the family's trepidation.

But Ivory and I had connected. He put his foot down and told his family that "Michael is my lawyer. That's it."

The law firm's founding partner also supported me. He liked me; he'd been the first to offer me the job. It was now my case. Either we'd win and catapult my career, or lose and I'd go back to being a nobody, the one who lost the big case—stressed at work, broke, nowhere.

At the time, the big legal "HMO" for many if not most of the cop unions in California was called the PORAC Legal Defense Fund (LDF). Officers and deputies paid dues to their unions. A small percentage of those dues were paid to LDF, which, when the officer or deputy needed, then provided an attorney to represent him or her. If it was a criminal charge where the conduct occurred on duty (as in Ivory's case and the bootcamp case), the law firm was paid through the LDF. If the misconduct occurred off duty, the deputy or officer would have to hire us, or any attorney for that matter, privately, out of their own pocket.

For administrative issues, LDF also covered the attorney costs.

As the case was national news, and would involve video and audio analyses, use of force analysis, and possibly even a behavioral psychologist (along with the other evidence, multiple witness statements/interviews, blood splatter analyses, etc.), the LDF authorized two attorneys on the case. Bill, my boss and supervisor, became my "second chair." It was awkward at first. Being the senior partner and name, high-profile cases historically always came to Bill. Ivory's case probably would've as well, had it not been Divine Providence that of all the attorneys in the office, I happened to be on call that morning and rolled out to the OIS. And like I said, Ivory and I had bonded.

Bill and I had different approaches. Work was important, but it was not my life; that was one part of the whole pie for me. My family and my religious and community life were my top priorities. I worked. I wasn't lazy. I must've studied that video literally a thousand, two thousand times. But I also lived outside the office.

An unplanned, unintentional competition soon formed. If I showed up at the office at 8:00 a.m. to start working on the case, he'd been there since 6:00 a.m. If I left at 6:00 p.m., he'd stay until 7:00 p.m.[24] He wasn't doing it on purpose; it was how he worked. [25] I was still the public defender; I worked up a case, but I didn't obsess over it. At that time, I had over 150 jury trials of experience guiding me to not obsess on a case. Remember, a trial is alive. It's three parts preparation and at least one part (and sometimes the percentages differ) tapping into that dynamic.

---

24 Although it may have gotten off to a rough start, working on the case together over the course of a year, Bill and I became less "boss to subordinate" and more colleague and friend.

25 At one point early on, the unspoken competition pushed me to seek out an old mentor of mine for advice. Bob Willey, may he rest in peace, was the assistant public defender for Riverside County, an experienced death penalty attorney, friend, and mentor. One afternoon, after an IA in Riverside, I found myself in his office, picking his brain about the dynamic. Bob was blunt, as usual. "It's your case," he smiled from across his desk. "You can collaborate, brainstorm, delegate. But a case can have only one first chair. You're it. Just have a frank, honest conversation. You're the captain. And you better do it now. The longer those roles aren't specifically delineated, the muddier the waters become. Ultimately, it'll damage your case and your client." I followed his advice and, although it was uncomfortable, had the conversation. Bill was a little taken aback at first, but quickly and professionally acknowledged my concerns and worked to allay them. In the end, a mutual respect and friendship formed. You may experience at some point, like I did, the need to work with a more senior attorney or boss on a case. Never forget, although collaboration and teamwork are obviously important, on your case you're the captain. It's your ship. Take charge. Your team will respect you for it. So will your client.

Connecting to that energy had become second nature to me; I thrived on it. I had an inner clock that told me when I'd spent enough time for the day. Moreover, having to live with the stress of having your boss be your "second chair," my other priorities helped keep me sane, whole.

I'd also learned, again, to roll with the evidence.

Early on, the LDF gave us a "blank check" to hire the best experts for the case. It was that big. Both of us were sure that if we could enhance the audio, Ivory must have said the word "Don't" before the ill-fated "Get up, get up" came out. But try as we might, expert after expert and hours of listening didn't turn up those four letters. I decided to give up on that approach and focus on a different but also common sense life-experience theory. Again, be flexible. Never get so emotionally tied to one theory or approach that you can't jettison it if it doesn't prove useful.

Don't Forget Your Life Experiences or Common Sense

As a kid, I was a huge fan of the old Abbot and Costello movies. To this day, the comedy genius of the two still makes me laugh. Sunday mornings in my house meant fresh rolls from the bakery, eggs, sometimes bagels, the Sports and Comics sections from the newspapers, and Abbot and Costello on the small, black-and-white screen in our kitchen. One recurring skit was Costello (the plump, funny one) becoming so afraid over something that, try as he might, he just couldn't speak. He would move his lips and make small sounds until, finally, half a sentence or even just one word managed to slip out. The old comedy routine clicked with me. Intense fear can and usually does stifle a person's ability to effectively articulate, even communicate. Ivory believed, based on all the circumstances, that he was confronting two violent, dangerous felons. Add to that divided attention—he had to keep one eye on the suspect on the ground by the passenger door, and one inside the dark car on the driver in the driver's seat. Alone, one of him against two of them, no idea if either or both were armed, and unfamiliar with where he was (the chase had led him into a neighboring city), Ivory was terrified. When the suspect on the ground put his hand seemingly into his jacket (it appeared that way on video) and said, "You better listen to me," Ivory was sure he was about to get shot. My theory, what I'd eventually argue and what the jury ultimately agreed with, was that in that intensely terrifying moment, we couldn't blame Ivory for being human, for maybe thinking but not articulating the "don't" before the "get up." It wasn't my whole argument, obviously, but it made sense to deflate that one, very bad sound bite. Again, in the context of the whole case, it made sense. And it worked.

To get there, we had to build a case, to get the jury to walk in his shoes, to feel Ivory's anxiety, his fear. One method I used was fast, rapid-fire cross-examination with the prosecution witnesses. Quick, sometimes even one-, two-, or three-worded questions kept the jury, and the witnesses on the edge of their seats. And it developed a rhythm—a fast, exciting but also anxious rhythm. The cross-examinations seemed to unfold rapidly. So did the events facing Ivory that night.

Another method was using the video as the best piece of evidence. Prosecution witnesses had given statements and testimony that sometimes contradicted the video. It's only natural. But now those contradictions would be impeached by the same video being used to prosecute Ivory. Turn the video into a tool and it loses its impact. It becomes just another piece of evidence, not the damning inhuman witness the prosecution was relying on.

As I've stated before, a trial has an energy. A dynamic you can feel. Sometimes it's obvious, sometimes it's nuanced. The more an attorney takes charge, the more that attorney influences that dynamic, and therefore the more credibility she or he has, which means, of course, the better the chance for a favorable outcome.

Having a different approach—changing the focus of our theory and defense—was never an issue. I'd learned to jettison, before it was too late, a theory that was simply not supported by the evidence. Smoking guns (no pun intended) are incredible when you have them. But you can't create one that isn't there. You need to deal with the evidence that you have.

Which gets back to preparation. Knowing your facts and the law guiding your case. Cold. In this case, the video coupled with the witness interviews were our facts. To create that fast-paced cross-examination, I couldn't be glued to my notes or a set of questions. When an attorney gets lost in his or her notes, the jury is lost too. Lose the jury, you lose your audience. You lose everything.

I studied the video. Day and night. And I hired a video-forensics expert, David Notowitz. Not only are four eyes better than two, but having someone who is objective and experienced in that field is an asset that if you can afford it, you need to procure.

It's Your Case, Choose Your Team: Sean Connery's Audition

When Ian Fleming's *James Bond* was targeted to make its big-screen debut back in the early sixties, the author of the popular spy series, Ian Fleming, had made it known that he was looking for a big name for the lead in the upcoming film: Cary Grant, James Mason, Trevor Howard. And he should know; who better than the character's creator to help decide the onscreen persona of the quintessential spy?

At the time, Sean Connery was a young, handsome actor who had yet to land a major movie role. A bodybuilder by trade, when he heard about the audition, he showed up unrehearsed, without any background or experience with the role. Without an agent. Nothing. He was on his way to watch a soccer game and parked at a meter thinking he'd duck in, quickly audition, and duck back out before his meter ran out. He wasn't expecting to land the role. It was on the way to the stadium. It was an audition of convenience.

The screen test took place in an upstairs hotel room in London. In the room were Connery and two producers. Connery was handed a script. Then, as described later by Connery himself, the actor proceeded to give an extremely poor audition. He left "knowing" that he was not getting the part. His soccer match awaited him.

After Connery walked out, the two producers may have laughed to themselves about the seemingly abysmal audition, but when they looked out the window, they noticed Sean Connery exiting the building downstairs and walking down the street. They watched him for a few minutes. Connery walked with his head high. Like he owned the street. Not arrogant, just self-confident. Unflustered by the horrible audition. They turned to each other and said firmly, "He's James Bond."

The Hollywood stars whom Fleming was eyeing were big names and would command big salaries. Sean Connery, by comparison, was a nobody. But he was a good-looking, self-confident, charismatic nobody who had all the right nuances to play the famous British spy with a license to kill. He got the part.

You'll notice a few themes running throughout this book, one being self-confidence. You need to believe in your abilities, your case, *you*! And you need to project that self-confidence to your audience, the jury. Poise and self-confidence are aspects of charisma. People are generally attracted to and gravitate toward self-confident, charismatic people. By projecting self-confidence, you'll be better able to connect to your jury. Connect and project.

Secondly, mistakes happen. Not every performance is perfect; many are far from it. Although you'll need to acknowledge mistakes made (and we all make them), acknowledge them privately, to yourself. Like the old commercial advised, "Never let them see you sweat." You'll make mistakes. Don't dwell on them; that will just compound the problem. Acknowledge them, learn from them, and move on. What many times seems to you to be a grave mistake didn't even register in the eyes of your audience, the jury. Acknowledge the mistake to yourself so you can do damage control, if necessary. Learn from it so you don't make the same mistake again. But then move on.

Finally, believe in yourself and your abilities. You can't win unless you believe you can. That's poise and self-confidence. People prefer to side with a winner, with a position of strength.

Apologists rarely win trials.

At the time, if I was a nobody in the cop-defense niche, David Notowitz was nonexistent in the forensic video analysis world. Trained in documentary films, having worked for a short time for the Financial News Network, and having received a Los Angeles Emmy award, David was more than knowledgeable in the field of film and video. But he was now married, with two kids, and needed to support his young family. So, although he took on commercial work every once in a while, videography—weddings, bar mitzvahs, sweet sixteens—became his bread and butter. His website boasted of the beautiful memories he'd created for families and friends.

When I announced to Bill and then to the LDF that, although we had the financial wherewithal to hire the "best in the country," I was choosing David, my credibility sunk further down the proverbial drain.

"Did you see his website?" the head of the LDF asked Bill in disbelief. "Weddings? Bar mitzvahs? Does Michael really know what he's doing?"

But I stuck to my guns. "He has a background in documentary film and news, which includes all kinds of footage, and he's intelligent, diligent, hardworking, and honest. I can work with him. He's my expert."

David soon became not only my video expert, but also a G-dsend.[26]

My next "pick" was a force expert. Again, we searched the field for available trainers, retired cops, you name it. Phone call after phone call to current clients, former clients, sergeants, lieutenants bore no fruit. We had the contacts, but couldn't find an expert to touch the case. Then I had an administrative case in Inglewood.

I was already very friendly with one of the captains. So, before my client's internal affairs interview, I stopped by the office and asked if the captain knew anyone. "Sgt. Kent Ferrin is our go-to guy" was the response. "That's funny," I mused out loud, "he just became a client of mine. That's who I'm here to see! We have his internal affairs interview in a couple of hours!" I walked back out to my car and pulled out the notebook on Ivory's case that I now took, and perused, everywhere I went. A few minutes later, I was talking to Kent in an interview room prepping for his IA.

His case was a run-of-the-mill citizen complaint from an arrestee, a convicted felon. Kent was being accused of rudeness. The entire contact was on audio. Kent had been more than professional. But a complaint was a complaint, so it had to be investigated. After we prepped for his interview, we had a few minutes to schmooze. I plopped my big notebook on the small, round Formica table. "Can I ask you about a case, no pressure?" I began. "I heard you're the go-to guy for use of force."

He shrugged and smiled. He explained that for the last few years he'd been teaching use of force in one of the Southern California police academies and around the South Bay to other agencies. I felt like I'd

---

26 The poetic irony is the case launched not only my career, but David's as well. He had the foresight to see he was talented at forensic analysis and changed his business model. Today he has one of the most sought-after, thriving forensic video and audio analysis shops in the country, The National Center for Audio and Visual Forensics (NCAVF).

again hit the jackpot. Tall, with a swimmer's build, blond hair, carved features, he looked like the Hollywood version of a stereotypical FBI agent. Kent Ferrin was a "Ken" doll embodied. If on top of that he was articulate and knowledgeable, the jury would love him.

He was.

They did.

Bill was again in disbelief. "Kent Ferrin," he asked incredulously.

"You know him?" I countered.

"I had him as a client years ago when he was with El Monte. He's a force expert?"

I became a little defensive. "They use him in Inglewood, and we both know how many IAs they have there for bopping people. I was told he's one of the South Bay's go-to guys. I like him, I think he's just what the doctor ordered. He's still a working stiff, still practicing what he's preaching. I think that makes a difference. And he's an intelligent, good-looking guy. I think the jury will like him too."

"He's a nice guy, but we can get anyone we want. You already picked David, the weddings/bar mitzvah guy. Don't you think a name, tried and true, is worth the money? It's beginning to look like amateur hour to the LDF. How much does he want, anyway?"

I smiled. "He's free. He just wants to help. It's not his day job."

We now had David and Kent on board. I was building *my* team. The last witness piece of the puzzle was Dr. Bill Lewinski, a behavioral psychologist from Minnesota State University who was *the* name in the industry. Charismatic, intelligent, likeable, his studies on action/ reaction, divided attention, and use of force had become legendary. He wasn't cheap. But he was *the* expert on this topic. He agreed to come on board as well to explain the human element of police officer training and use of force. Lastly, our investigator, Tom Crompton, was recommended to me from a seasoned defense attorney in Riverside. Smart, affable, diligent, and hard-working, Tom would work out so well that he'd become my investigator on all my cases for the next fifteen years. And not to forget our paralegal extraordinaire, Cheryl Mitchell.

We had our team.

When the case calls for it, an attorney needs to be willing to reach out, to build a team. It may be expert witnesses, paralegal assistants, investigators, other attorneys. The key is not how big a name is, although obviously experience helps. But just like a sports team, a team of all-stars is not always a winning combination. How well you all work together if you're on the same page—or if on different pages, that those pages complement each other—is the key. Some of the best championship teams didn't have a lineup of individual all-stars. But together, they were just the right mix to win.

By the same point, the lead attorney is the captain of the ship. You can have a first mate, a great crew each with different roles and responsibilities, but the lead attorney needs to *lead*. Don't rely too much on any one member of the team—all the moving parts still need a captain to guide and steer the ship. Without a captain and a plan, even the best crew can be swept from current to current without ever reaching their destination. In trial work, reaching your destination means winning your case.

Sure, don't micromanage, but be the captain.

Knowing Your Facts: Witness Statements

Some people are visually oriented, some audibly. Some have a penchant for both. Witness interviews are routinely recorded and transcribed. Depositions are now not only memorialized in transcripts, but many are also video and audio recorded as well. If you're visually oriented, then the traditional reading, analyzing, and outlining of the transcripts is what has and still works for you. If you're more audibly oriented, like me, listening to the interviews ingrains them into memory better than a cold read and outlining. I use both methods, as, obviously, at some point you may have to confront the witness with a transcript during cross-examination (or refresh their memory during direct), so having an outline with page and line references is integral. But to know their statements, one or two readings and your notes or outlines really isn't going to cut it. I listen to witness interviews and recorded testimony almost *ad nauseum*. More than just what they said, you get a much better sense of how they said it and who they are. Their tone of voice, inflection, pregnant or nervous pauses. It all goes into the mix. And the more I listen, the more I *know* my facts.

In the bootcamp case, I must have listened to Detective Smith's interview of Jane Doe #2 literally a couple dozen times. Sure, I ended up taking notes and outlining the transcript. But when Smith took the stand and started testifying, I *knew* what Jane Doe #2 had said, literally word for word. Which meant I also knew what she *didn't* say. I didn't need to be studying a transcript all throughout the detective's testimony. Instead, I studied *him*.

While I'm in the car driving, in the grocery store, or washing dishes in the kitchen, I've got my AirPods in and I'm listening to a witness interview, recorded testimony. By the time I'm outlining a transcript, it's really just a matter of recording the page and line of what I know I already need. It's an efficient way to use "downtime."

And it works.

In Ivory's case, I listened to those witness interviews literally dozens of times. By the time trial came, I not only knew the interviews, I also *knew* those witnesses—their voices, inflections, reactions. They were familiar to me now. And that familiarity translated into a level of comfort during cross-examination that was felt by the jury, by everyone in the courtroom.

The same can be said of the video. The visuals, the verbal exchanges. It was almost like a zen thing—it all became a part of my psyche. Any deviation, therefore, was sensed before ever having to flip a page or rewind a video.

When you do outline your witness transcripts or reports, another trick straight from law school is to outline them more than once, each time narrowing it down to the finer points. It's another method of knowing your facts and focusing on the meat and potatoes. I find it much easier to examine witnesses with outlines and bullet points than actual questions. Bullet points give you the freedom to be flexible in wording your questions, and the ability to simply take a quick, reminder glance down to your outline to keep on track. Questions are inflexible and claustrophobic, and they necessitate reading the actual question, which usually means longer than a quick glance. Again, it affects the presentation, the jury's perception of your preparation, knowledge, and self-confidence, and gives the witness time to regroup. Bullet points and outlines are much more liberating.

"Client Control": Managing Expectations

Between the ages of eighteen and twenty-four, I worked full time and part time for a contractor specializing in kitchens. The owner, an old Italian guy named "Ray," treated me well. His older son was my immediate boss. My partner was the boss's younger son, "Anthony." I started the job while I was in college; Anthony was several years older than me and in dental school. He looked and sounded like Billy Crystal and had the intelligence and sense of humor to match.

We hit it off immediately.

The company generally, and Anthony and I in particular, did good work. The real issues were timing and expectations. Ray always took on more work than he had employees to handle it, which meant that each project was always late. Late in starting the project, late in finishing the project. Customers would call, complaining. Ray routinely told them to let his "workers know," which meant that Anthony's and my job duties usually included being the verbal punching bags for the customer's justified frustration.

I really couldn't say anything, but Anthony could. We'd come back from a job and Ray would ask how it went. His son would smile a sarcastic smile and quote the customer's tirade almost verbatim. Ray would shrug, smile, and ask, "Well, did he pay you?"

Anthony would then explode. "Pay us? We're two weeks late on what we promised! And it's not done! I'm not going to ask him for money until we finish; he's already paid us half. The other half is due . . . upon completion!" By this point I was usually standing by the fridge in the office, grabbing a drink, smirking to myself.

"Dad," he'd continue, "why can't you just give them a conservative time estimate in the first place? Instead of four weeks, tell them six weeks! So they know what to expect? If we finish in four, we're heroes. If we finish in six, we kept our word. It's kinda simple." And so it went, as regular as clockwork, week after week, for the almost six years I worked there.

Ray would try to lecture Anthony about "customer control." In the legal profession, the phrase commonly bantered around is "client control." I could never stand either phrase. They sound arrogant, as if our clients are chattel, not people. If I've used it here and there, it was probably because I was too lazy or too reluctant to correct someone using the phrase in a conversation with me. My bad. Sincerely. "Client control" speaks of a lack of empathy for your client. We work in a service profession.

In reality, the phrase really means "managing expectations." It usually pops up in a conversation regarding either opposing counsel's impatience with the timing or scheduling of the case, a client's seeming obstinacy with an offer to settle, or both. But what it really means is the client's expectations about the case, or what he or she wants as an outcome, is unrealistic. It usually boils down to the attorney not taking the time to instill in her or his client reasonable expectations, which should be done as soon as possible and revisited semi-often. Unreasonable expectations can easily lead to dissatisfied and disgruntled clients, poor attorney-client relationships, and an inability to make solid, informed decisions within the litigation of the case.

Yes, it all sounds bad.

Too often, attorneys think they need to build confidence with their client by either building false expectations or reinforcing her or his client's unrealistic ones. Both are recipes for failure. No attorney needs to be Eeyore from Winnie the Pooh. But infusing a dose of reality into your representation and communications with your client helps them expect the worst while always hoping for the best. No one can then ever complain, "You never told me this would happen," or "I would've never hired you if you would've told me that." It helps dramatically in settlement discussions if your client has already been primed for the best- and worst-case scenarios and everything in between, including not only the strengths of their case but its weaknesses as well. And their own personal strengths and weaknesses. Some people simply can't afford to go to trial, either financially or emotionally. By controlling expectations, your settlement and strategic discussions will be much more meaningful and productive.

I acknowledge with my clients in the first or second meeting that trusting a lawyer seems like an oxymoron. But the reality is, if they don't trust their lawyer, they have no business hiring you in the first place. An attorney-client relationship is just that: *a relationship*. And like any relationship, it's built and survives on mutual trust. The components of that are respect and honesty. Any relationship without mutual respect and honesty has no trust. Without trust, there is no relationship.

Your client doesn't have to love you or even like you (although, hopefully they do). *But they must trust you.* Respect you. Without that, the representation suffers, the case suffers, everything suffers.

I usually prime my clients with the weaknesses of their case from day one, telling them I'm playing devil's advocate to make sure there are no surprises. I warn them that for the length of my representation they will hear more bad news than good. Again, I prime them that I'm trying to stay three steps ahead of the opposing attorney. Litigation is chess, not checkers. Good chess players think at least three, four, or even more moves ahead of the move they're making at that moment. Not just a plan—but one move, two moves, their opponent's possible moves/strategy, counter moves, potential traps, and land mines, etc. And they're thinking that far out for *each and every move.*

If I were opposing counsel, how would I litigate this case? What would be my plan, my strategy? How would I use this piece of evidence or deflate that witness? When I play devil's advocate, and I do it a lot, I make sure my client knows that I'm doing that for *their* benefit. Surprises during litigation or trial lead to losses (Unless they're good surprises!). No client or attorney likes losing. Finally, I pound home that my only concern is zealously representing *them*—not their employer, spouse, friend, parent, all the people that seem to have more than two cents worth of advice and criticism. Those people may mean well, but the client hired me, not them. And my job, the oath I took as an attorney, was to honor that trust and that confidence fully.

Ivory was the perfect client. He trusted me implicitly. I trusted I could be less than the bluebird of happiness when discussing his case and the surrounding politics, public and professional, that influenced its filing and prosecution. He trusted that I was putting everything I had into defending him, which I was. It created an attorney-client bond that strengthened everything about our defense. Remember, it's their case and their life. The real operative phrase is not "client control" but "managing expectations."

Little Picture: Details, Details, Details

Leave the gun. Take the cannoli.

—CLEMENZA, FRANCIS FORD COPPOLA'S THE GODFATHER

So now you've got an outline of your closing argument, you're building client trust, you know the jury instructions/law you're dealing with, you're absorbing the facts, and you're managing expectations.

Great. Fabulous.

Don't forget the details—even the mundane, obvious details.

In what many audiences consider one of the best movies ever made, perhaps the most memorable line was not in the script. Richard S. Castellano, the actor who played mob capo Peter Clemenza, was the son of Italian immigrants. In one scene in the movie, Clemenza leaves his house early to go to "work." When his wife walks out the front door to ask him where he's going, he tells her he might be back late. She reminds him as he's getting in the car, "Don't forget the cannoli." The movie then fades into later that day and the real purpose for the car ride: the murder of Paulie, the Godfather's traitorous driver. Clemenza, already out of the car when the murder takes place (they had parked on the side of a remote stretch of road for him to relieve himself, which he was doing when the shot rang out), is soon joined by his accomplice. His partner asks Clemenza what he should do about the murder weapon?

Matter-of-factly, Castellano, the actor, improvised one of the most famous lines in movie history: "Leave the gun. Take the cannoli."[27]

A small detail, sure, but one that gave depth and realism to the character, the culture, the entire movie. And it's still remembered fifty years later.

Like a digital photograph made up of tiny little pixels, trials are also made up of small, significant details. Big picture/little picture. The details are the pixels, the "little picture."

---

27 "Leave the gun" was in the script. "Take the cannoli" was ad-libbed.

"Zipper Your Fly"

Every prosecutor, besides the actual elements of the crime he or she needs to prove, must prove up jurisdiction. It's not a given. Every case must have affirmative evidence that the crime took place within the court's jurisdiction. It's usually asked in the very beginning of the first witness's testimony. It may seem mundane, basic. But it's an element in every single case.

In my early public defender days, trying a misdemeanor 148 (violation of California Penal Code 148—resisting, obstructing, or delaying a peace officer during the course and scope of his or her duties) was David vs. Goliath. Every time. Ventura was an ultraconservative county that stood 100% behind law enforcement. A 148 "charge" against your client was as good as a 148 "conviction." As one judge with a smirk put it in master calendar court when sending out a defendant and his attorney to trial on a 148, "You're assigned to department 33 for trial and sentencing."

I had lost my first 148 case, a case where my client had run from the police after ditching some beer (he was under the age of 21) and was summarily "disciplined" for doing so. I was determined not to lose a 148 again. And I didn't.

The first one I won involved a 19-year-old client. "Johnny" was a new father. He had decided to break up with his girlfriend, the mother of his child, because he felt she was too unstable. One day, he went to her parents' house, where she and the baby were living, to let her know and discuss custody and visitation. He was a community college student, smart, responsible. That Tuesday afternoon he broke the news.

She didn't take it so well.

She flew off the handle, locked herself and the baby in her parents' bedroom, and threatened to kill herself. My client knew her father owned a gun.

He went into the kitchen, picked up the phone, and called 911. Describing the situation, he also described his fear that she may carry out her threat. The local police department was dispatched, which, hearing that a gun was involved, set up a perimeter and ordered both out of the house. Johnny was still on the phone with 911 and tried to explain he couldn't make her exit; she had locked herself in the room. That's why he'd called 911. But they insisted he come out with her. The standoff lasted about an hour.

Seeing it was going nowhere, Johnny took the phone into the garage and opened the garage door so the officers could see him. They could, although he couldn't see them. They ordered him out of the garage, but he said he didn't want to leave her in the house locked in the room with their baby and a gun. He lifted his shirt to show he had no weapon. The officers weren't satisfied. Meanwhile, his girlfriend got on the phone as well. Slowly but surely, the 911 operator talked her into leaving the room and coming outside too. Now they were both in the garage. Johnny walked slowly from the garage to the driveway with his hands on his head. Once on the driveway, his girlfriend also began to walk out of the garage. Soon they were on the driveway, hands on their heads. An officer approached them. Then two officers. They were patted down, then told to sit down. Johnny's girlfriend sat down, but then Johnny remembered. "My baby," he said, and turned to go back into the house. An officer, fearing he was going inside to get a weapon, grabbed him and threw him onto the ground. He suffered a bloody nose and an arrest for 148.

It was a stupid case. We tried to get the DA to dismiss it, but it was too political. The police department never agreed to dismissing 148s, and the DA's office never wanted to rock that political boat. So, we went to trial.

The DA put on only two witnesses, two of the officers that had been on the scene and had arrested Johnny. We had stipulated to the 911 call. Photos of the scene came into evidence through the officers. After the second cop testified, the DA rested his case.

In criminal court in California, after the prosecution rests, the defense can make a motion under Penal Code section 1118.1, arguing that there has not been enough evidence presented of one or more of the elements for the case to go forward to the jury. In nearly 27 years, I've only seen a handful granted, and usually only if there were multiple counts charged and the motion was for only several or one of those counts. Judges are reluctant to take a case away from a jury. So, after the second officer left the courtroom and the DA rested, the judge turned to me and asked if I had any witnesses?

I responded, "I'd like to make a 1118.1 motion to dismiss, Your Honor." I could tell the judge was about to summarily deny it when I continued. "The prosecutor never proved up jurisdiction, Your Honor."

The judge looked stunned for a moment, then sat back and scratched his head. He looked down at his notes for another moment, and then back up with a smirk, a very mischievous smirk.

He turned toward the DA.

"He's right. You never asked it."

The prosecutor took a big gulp and meekly asked if he could reopen. The judge said yes, turned, and told the bailiff to see if the cop was still in courthouse. He was. The judge told the jury to take a break while we waited for the officer to return.

Then, outside the presence of the jury but in open court (but off the record), the judge turned back to the DA and began, "You know, Mr. 'Jones,' asking about jurisdiction is like, well . . . It's like during the break, you go to the bathroom. When you're done urinating, you turn, go to the sink, wash your hands, and walk out. But you forgot to zip your fly. So you come into court after the break with your fly open.

"Forgetting to ask the jurisdiction question for a DA, Mr. Jones, is like forgetting to zip your fly. And right now," and the judge leaned forward, smiling even more mischievously, "your fly is open. Don't forget to zip your fly again!"

He put the officer back on and asked him the two questions for jurisdiction. Then we called my client to testify.

We rested, and after closing arguments the jury was sent back to deliberate. I hadn't even made it down the hallway when the bailiff opened the doors to the courtroom and yelled for us to come back.

In just seven minutes the jury had acquitted my client!

Sure, we felt vindicated by the win. But that exchange by the judge and the DA . . . CLASSIC!

Details, details, details.

Trial Judo

It can't be said enough—spend time going over the discovery and the evidence, over and over again. Key pieces of evidence, especially ones at the center of the case, never get old. It's like looking at a complex painting—the more you study it, the more things you see. Especially with video or any visual evidence. Be it the timing, lighting, angles, multiple actions going on, lens, system it was recorded on . . . the more you look, the more you see. And what may have seemed like a bad piece of evidence, or a bad fact, can be flipped on its head.

The prosecution in the Ivory Webb case made it no secret—their theory of the case was that Ivory was angry, out of control, and he shot the passenger out of that anger. One bad fact in the video (among a few) was near the beginning of the exchange between Ivory and the airman. There was a glaring white flash on the video, followed by Ivory kicking at the airman and yelling, "Get the fuck on the ground!" He looked angry, mean. I knew that visual was good ammunition for the prosecution in the opening statement, closing argument, you name it.

One afternoon, while David and I were again viewing the video ad nauseum, David turned to me very casually and asked, "Would you like to see what's behind the white flash?" I was shocked. "You can do that?! Isn't that flash Ivory's flashlight blinding the camera lens?"

David chuckled. "No. Whoever was working the camera touched a filter by mistake. I can find a filter that can minimize the effect and let us see the action that was whited out . . . if you want."

I smiled and nearly screamed, "Well . . . YEAH!!!"

A few minutes later, after playing with different filters, we saw what was behind the flash. The airman had begun to get up! He was nearly three-quarters standing up, one hand grabbing on to the open passenger door, in complete defiance of Ivory's commands to stay on the ground. What had seemed like a malicious kick, for no reason, was really a reaction to the suspect standing up in defiance of Ivory's direct orders to stay on the ground. The kick, once a bad fact, now looked completely reasonable!

David quickly created a version of the video that filtered out the white flash. It was included in our discovery that we turned over to the prosecution more than a month before trial, along with other versions, some loops of actions, slow motions, and close-ups.[28]

Another creation we produced were loops of video that stopped right on the frames that depicted how close the airman's hands came to

---

28 An interesting tidbit: the prosecution had sent the video, including the whited-out part, to the FBI in Quantico as well as NASA, for analysis. Neither agency did what David did—use a filter to uncover what had occurred during the whited-out section of the video.

Ivory's weapon. On at least two separate occasions, the airman reached out in front of himself with an open hand coming literally within inches of Ivory's pointed gun. The airman was probably trying to shield his eyes from Ivory's flashlight. But in the heat of the standoff, from a completely different perspective, Ivory wouldn't know that. It would seem to him that the suspect was reaching for his gun. By demonstrating how close he came, we could argue (along with other evidence) that the video did *not* illustrate an angry, out of control deputy but, on the contrary, a scared, extremely restrained law enforcement officer trying his best while handling two dangerous suspects. What was once a horrible piece of evidence, a video seemingly showing my client out of control, was slowly becoming our best asset.

Sure, it doesn't always work out that way. But not panicking, keeping an open mind, and really digging into the evidence can often lead to the above situations, especially with technology-based evidence. I call it trial judo—taking what seems to be a bad fact or bad piece of evidence and channeling it into a positive.

Be it video, audio, documentation—it's all evidence. Evidence is a legal name for a tool. It can be a tool to prove an element or deflate one. To build credibility or destroy it. But it's a tool, nonetheless. When viewed in that light, a "bad" video or a "bad" witness may not always ruin your case. Especially when turned on its head and used to help your case. Like a slingshot, being able to utilize to your advantage what seemed to be a negative piece of evidence when you first got the case or at the beginning of the trial strengthens your point/position, while weakening the other side. The paradox is powerful. A good fact is always more potent when gleaned on cross-examination (when possible) than on direct. David's revelation was described by jurors afterward as a turning point in how they viewed the video. And once we turned that proverbial corner, the momentum just kept building.

Supplies

That summer years ago, Joey and I didn't set sail without first checking that everything on the boat was in order and working properly. And of course, not without a case of beer (we *were* twenty-four). We had a general handle on the weather, the currents, and boat traffic. We felt prepared.

In trial, I make sure I have enough supplies on hand that it's almost like carrying a mini office in a box. Plenty of pads (notepads, not iPads, although if that's your preference, go for it), pens, highlighters, Post-its in different sizes, even paper clips. I also have a pad, pen, and a set of Post-its for my client, whom I tell before court during our preparation that if they want to tell me something, write it down and let me see it, don't talk or whisper to me. First, the microphone may pick up the conversation. Second, I need to hear what's going on. I can take a quick glance at a note on a Post-it or pad and still listen. At the end of each trial day, I put all the notes my client wrote into my supplies box to take with me (i.e., they stay confidential). Although in almost thirty years I've never had an issue, for those whose paranoia has started to kick in while reading this, just have your client write at the top of the page "ATTORNEY-CLIENT PRIVILEGE." A Post-it note your client hands you directly is obviously a confidential attorney-client communication.

Lastly, and again very practically, I bring a case of water. You're there all day. On some days, you'll be doing a good amount of the speaking. You'll get thirsty. Getting through a cross-examination or closing argument with a dry mouth is not fun. A case of water may sound like too much to lug to court, but most judges allow you to keep your stuff in the court overnight while you're in trial, so you're only lugging it once. As the trial wears on, you'll thank yourself for bringing it. So will your client.

PREPARATION
Compass Points

. . .

A. **Self-confidence—You can't win unless you believe you can**
B. **Influences in and out of Court**
   - Don't Forget Your Common Life Experiences or Common Sense—your narrative and evidence need to make sense and speak to your audience
   - It's Your Case, Choose Your Team
C. **Know Your Facts—COLD**
   - Witness statements
   - Video evidence
   - Audio evidence
   - Documentary evidence
   - Photographs
D. **"Client Control"—Managing Expectations**
E. **Little Picture: Details, Details, Details**
F. **Trial Judo: turning "bad" facts into good facts**
G. **Supplies**

CHAPTER FOUR

IN THE HEAT
OF BATTLE

Nine-tenths of wisdom is being wise in time.
—THEODORE ROOSEVELT

We just spoke about not overlooking details. Don't let your client overlook them, either. But, more importantly, *don't overlook your clients!* Every attorney develops her or his own style, including how well she or he works with clients. I try to work closely with my clients. It's their lives, after all. And I try to make sure that I pick their brains for details when I can and when it seems to be productive.

Factual details are one thing. We've talked about them and will talk about them some more. But there are other details to trial work that can only come with experience and preparation. Knowing the evidence code, basic points like laying foundations for evidence, proper and sustainable objections, when to object (and when not to), how to impeach a witness—these are skills learned while in the heat of battle. You can read books on sailing but until you experience the feel of the sail catching and holding the wind, of jibbing or tacking to shift course, you're a student, not a sailor. I can (and will) try to give you a good overview, examples, and advice, but some things really take hold only when applied and experienced.

Objections and Foundations

Speculation. One of the most common objections is probably "speculation." Ironically, if you look in the evidence code, it is *not* a delineated objection. It's really shorthand for "the answer is irrelevant because there is no foundation that the witness has personal knowledge and is therefore giving an improper opinion."[29] But judges and attorneys over the years became used to the shortened, less cumbersome version of simply "calls for speculation." It's a justified objection whenever the foundation has not been laid that the witness has personal knowledge of what's being asked within the question. If a judge overrules it, you can follow up with the actual, proper objection—"objection, relevance, lack of foundation, no personal knowledge." What that really means is "Your Honor, what, were you asleep? She never laid the foundation that this witness knows anything about this." And the way to get around such an objection is simply to rephrase the question, adding "to your knowledge" or "if you know."

Foundation—the most misunderstood building block.

- Hearsay
  - ✓ *Business records and documentation*

Many lawyers think that simply asking the one question is enough foundation. Some judges agree. Obviously, they're wrong. Lazily asking, "Did you create this document in the normal course and scope of your employment?" seems to address a business record exception to the hearsay rule. But the proper way to do it is to establish the witness's position/job, his or her job duties, the witness's personal knowledge of such a document, the witness's knowledge of how such a record is normally created, what role the witness normally has in such a document's creation, what role the witness had in this particular document's creation or production, and was this document, then, created within the normal course and scope of the witness's employment, as has just been described. Now you've laid a foundation.

By the same token, an experienced judge will make an attorney, upon objection, lay a proper foundation. And believe it

---

29 Which is really a foundation objection, in sheep's clothing!

or not, many attorneys, even seasoned ones, never being called on the carpet, when put to the task have a hard time doing it. It's the objection that time and again gets the most mileage. This includes photographs as well. The attorney should not be explaining to the witness and the court what's depicted in a photo or document, and then asking the witness to identify it or testify about it. The lawyer is the one testifying to the foundation, not the witness. Lawyers ask questions of witnesses; they don't testify for them (At least they're not supposed to!). It's very bad form. Put the photograph in front of the witness. Identify it by the evidence number or letter ("plaintiff's exhibit 1 for identification," "defense exhibit A for identification"), and then ask the witness if he or she recognizes it or what is depicted therein. If the answer is yes, ask the witness to describe it. You've now laid a proper foundation. The same is true for medical records, business records, or any form of documentation. Even videos. It is for the witness to identify the evidence, not the lawyer. Conversely, when the lawyer does testify for the witness, it deserves an objection (Unless it becomes so boring that they seem to be losing the jury. In that case, let them.).

Remember, no evidence can come into trial without laying some foundation for its relevance and, depending on the evidence, authenticity. Documents are inherently hearsay—out-of-court statements offered for the truth of the matter asserted within them. Things like medical records, business records (yes, also the name of the exception) are all hearsay unless the proper foundation is laid. In fact, even direct testimony many times drifts into hearsay without a proper foundation. Why? Either the information being offered fits into an exception, or it is not being offered for the truth of the matter asserted within the statement and, therefore, is not hearsay.

✓ *State of mind/future actions*

You learned this in evidence in law school: hearsay is an out-of-court statement that is being offered for the truth of the matter asserted *within that statement*. The robotic retort most attorneys spew out when opposing counsel makes a hearsay objection is, "It's not being offered for the truth of the matter asserted [within the statement]." They don't claim it's an exception; it's just not hearsay. I'll often argue that if it's not an exception, and not being offered for the truth of the matter asserted in the statement, then it's not relevant, either. Again, the usual retort to that is it's being offered to explain why the witness did what he or she did next, or his or her state of mind. My retort to that is that we can easily get there by simply asking the witness the question about what he or she did next, or how he or she was feeling or thinking, without the hearsay statement. Sometimes the judge agrees, sometimes she doesn't. If the statement does come in, albeit "not for the truth of the matter asserted," you can request that the judge admonish the jury right then and there that they are *not* to consider such evidence for its truth, but only to establish the witness's state of mind or explain his or her subsequent actions. If you don't receive that, at least make sure you request and receive the jury instruction that states that certain evidence came in for a limiting purpose, in this case to prove state of mind or explain actions.

✓ *Bias*

One exception to hearsay is impeachment. Be it a prior inconsistent statement or bias, impeaching a witness with his or her prior statements or documentation that contradicts their current testimony is almost always admissible as an exception to hearsay. But you still need to lay a proper foundation.

Even obvious bias needs more than just "Didn't you tell so-and-so you would get even with my client?" Sure, the question seems like fair game on the surface. But a past, out-of-court statement is still hearsay. And the form of the question will be objected to as argumentative (most impeachment is; it's the nature of the beast), and most judges will sustain such an objection. But if the question is preceded by a foundation, a series of questions that establish the bias or the circumstances of the relevance, credibility, and then obvious bias of the witness who made the prior statement, you've laid a proper foundation. Within that foundation or series of questions, the witness usually has given you a denial or contradiction that will help paint them into a corner further into the examination. But by working up to the impeachment incrementally, gradually, once you get there, it becomes not only much more obvious but also more powerful. So if you get a sustained objection for lack of foundation, don't stress. Maybe you can overcome it, maybe not. Stop. Think. Remember, trial judo. Sometimes even a sustained objection for lack of foundation, causing you to regroup and, to be blunt, do it right, is a gift not a hinderance.

"Randy"

"Randy" was an out-of-work mechanic—a very large, muscular, out-of-work mechanic. He'd gotten into a labor dispute with his boss who, after Randy demanded the overtime pay he was entitled to, summarily fired him. Randy filed a case with the National Labor Relations Board (NLRB) and was in the throes of its investigation into his claim, when he decided that maybe he could just settle the dispute man-to-man. So, one night he visited his former employer right after his boss had closed the shop. As was likely to happen, his boss, Steve, refused to pay him what he owed and, instead, picked up a broomstick and swung it wildly at Randy. Randy took a step back, avoided the stick, then summarily, instinctively slapped his former boss in the face, causing his boss to drop the stick. The slap, more embarrassing than painful, caused some redness to his assailant's cheek, but that's it. Randy turned around, got in his car, and drove home to his one-room trailer. Tired and frustrated, he cracked open a beer and called his girlfriend.

About an hour later, there was a loud knock at his door followed by an even louder "Sheriff's department, we have a warrant for your arrest!" Randy looked out his window and saw two Ventura County sheriff's vehicles, lights flashing, parked within about twenty feet of his trailer. He opened his door, came out, and was ordered onto the ground at gunpoint. When he asked why, he was told he was being arrested for a felony assault with a deadly weapon, a knife. Randy looked up and saw his old boss pointing at him from behind one of the patrol cars, smiling. Randy knew no knife had been involved. His boss had lied. Now he was being arrested for a serious felony.

Randy claimed, and I believed him, that if he really had wanted to beat up his old boss, who was literally almost half his size, his boss would have suffered more than just some redness on his cheek. He also swore there had never been a knife.

Somewhere along the way, while the case was pending, Randy's boss admitted in an interview that he might have been "mistaken" about the knife, but he was still adamant that Randy had battered him. The deadly weapon charge was dropped, but the battery and resisting arrest charges weren't. We continued the case, several times trying to get some records from Arizona showing that the boss had given false information on a driver's license application. Arizona DMV claimed it could not find the record. The master calendar court judge was growing impatient with me. "This is your last continuance, I'm making a note in the court file," he threatened. Walking out of the courtroom, Randy turned to me. "I got a voice mail from Steve where he threatens to have me arrested, even falsely, if I don't drop the NLRB case. Would that be relevant?"

I stopped, looked him in the face (actually, looked *up* at his face) and said, "Uh, YEAH, where is it??!!"

"I have it at home. Should I bring it to your office?"

I smiled. "I want it this afternoon at the latest!"

That afternoon, Randy showed up with the tape. Sure enough, it was his boss threatening that he had connections, that he gave to the DA's campaign, and he could make up any story to have Randy arrested if Randy didn't drop his claim. The kicker: the date on the recording was two days before the incident.

This is rare: almost never does an attorney really get such a smoking gun to use to impeach a witness. Good facts sometimes, yes. Good cross-examinations, yes. But a real smoking gun? Now a trial that I'd dreaded couldn't happen fast enough. I must've listened to that tape a thousand times, each time my smile getting bigger.

Some attorneys might have given the tape to the prosecutor, and I usually do give them everything up front. But I felt that the recording would destroy the battery charge and, seeing that, the prosecutor would then probably dismiss the battery but still go forward on the 148/ resisting arrest. I wanted both. I reasoned that if the jury saw what a piece of work Randy's boss was, and how he'd obviously framed Randy (first a knife that wasn't there, then a battery, preceded by a threat to falsely accuse him), I could argue that Randy had been innocent, falsely accused, and was now being arrested for crimes he did not commit by the same boss who had threatened to do just that—he was emotional, angry, and it seemed, justifiably so. When the deputy was processing him, Randy presented as a huge, over-six-foot-tall, angry, violent felony suspect. The deputy would naturally be more guarded and nervous when dealing with this large, muscular, angry suspect. Both men, then, emotional for different reasons, overreacted to each other. Neither was wrong. Both were human. It was a misunderstanding, as happens in life. But it was just that, and nothing more. Two human beings being human. And so, no crime (i.e., no resisting arrest) was committed, either. That would be my argument. I needed the battery and the related impeachment to make that case really hit home. I couldn't risk the DA dismissing the battery, in effect dismissing my impeachment of Steve. So I didn't tell the prosecutor about the tape.[30]

We started trial. After picking a jury (in Ventura in those days, that took less than a day), Randy's boss, Steve, was the first witness. On direct, he played the victim. The DA even tried to deflate his original false claim of a knife by having him admit to it on direct. His excuse: he was terrified of Randy and "thought" he'd had a knife but, reflecting on it afterward, he "realized" he'd never actually seen a knife, so felt he had to "make the prosecutor aware of that" after Randy had been charged. It was one of those times that I thought to myself "And they say defense attorneys are slimy? How can the prosecutor buy this garbage?" The more he testified, the more antsy I got to impeach him.

Finally, cross-exam. It began purposely benign. I asked him basic questions about his professional relationship with Randy, his shop, the layout, hours, the last time Randy had actually worked for him, etc. I asked him about the NLRB claim. He dismissed it as being specious, but it was an obvious sore point. Then I went into the night in question. Point by point. Detail by detail. He made a mistake here, a contradiction there,

---

30 The case law states unequivocally that impeachment evidence of an opposing side's witness need not be turned over until the witness testifies.

but defensively stuck to his guns that Randy had been the aggressor, he the victim. Then came the question.

"Isn't it true, that on a voice mail message you threatened my client with false prosecution if he didn't drop the NLRB claim?" Truth is, I was still a new, less experienced attorney when this trial took place. Even though I expected the prosecutor to object, I didn't expect the judge to sustain her objection!

"Counsel, approach," the judge growled, visibly annoyed.

"Your Honor," the DA said at the sidebar, "we were never provided this voice mail. It's a violation of 1054."

"No, it's not, Your Honor," I countered. "The case law is pretty unequivocal—"

"Sustained," the old judge bellowed angrily, cutting me off. "Sustained! You can get it in through your client, if you lay a foundation, but not him!"

I walked back to counsel table, angry, frustrated, a little at a loss. It was obvious impeachment. It should come in *through this witness!*

I looked at the witness. He was sneering. He thought he'd won, again.

He wouldn't.

I was determined.

The bottom line is I needed to lay a better foundation. Once I had worked up to the voice mail, laying the foundation with questions that demonstrated Steve's bias, I had enough to ask him about the voice mail. If he agreed he'd sent it, then he's effectively impeached, albeit not as powerfully as I'd wanted. To play the tape, then, may have necessitated it coming in through my client's testimony. But if he denied sending it, playing it would be playing a prior inconsistent statement—his denial would be a foundation for the hearsay exception. If he didn't remember (which was ultimately what he testified to), then playing it would be refreshing recollection, again, an exception.

Thinking on my feet, I regrouped. "Mr. Smith," I began, "you strongly disagreed with my client's NLRB claim, didn't you?"

"Yes."

"Made you angry he was claiming back wages he wasn't entitled to, didn't it?"

"Damn right!"

"Thought he was trying to rip you off?"

"Yes."

"Made you so angry you made up a false accusation of my client threatening you with a knife, just to have him arrested?"

"That was a mistake!"

I looked him in the eye, took out a mini cassette recorder, put it on the edge of the table, and put my hand on it. "Are you sure? Do you recall leaving my client a voice mail message, angry at his NLRB claim, two days before his arrest, threatening to have him falsely arrested if he didn't drop it?" I tapped on the mini cassette recorder.

Now he looked nervous. No more sneer. Before the DA could object, he blurted out, "I don't remember."

I smiled. "Would it *refresh your memory* to hear the recording of you threatening my client with false prosecution?"

He squirmed, then almost squeaked, "It might."

I looked at the judge, barely able to hide my smirk. He was angry but helpless.

"Play the tape," the judge almost snarled.

I did. With a smile, all the while staring right at Steve.

Listening to his recorded threat, the jury stared at him too. Like he was the devil. After the recording finished, I asked him, "That was your voice, wasn't it?"

"Yes," was his soft reply.

"That refresh your memory, that you threatened my client with false prosecution two days before his arrest if he didn't drop the NLRB claim?"

"Yes," was another soft reply.

"No further questions at this time, Your Honor."

I argued in closing just what I'd described above, that given the circumstances, my client being arrested for a violent felony he knew he hadn't committed, accused by a slimy, lying ex-boss who had threatened to have him falsely arrested and had made good on his promise, Randy was reasonably upset by the situation and would have a hard time not demonstrating that frustration during his arrest.

On the other hand, the deputy knew none of this. All the deputy knew was that Randy was a big, muscular felony suspect who seemed angry and therefore dangerous. It was a bad combination, but a very human one. So when Randy, while going through the booking process, turned angrily with a pen in hand to ask a question, the deputy reacted in step and took what he thought was a violent, resistive suspect to the ground, subsequently charging him with resisting arrest. But Randy hadn't really resisted anything. He was just acting very human, under the circumstances.

The jury agreed. Not guilty on all counts.

Like I said above, most juries view trials as morality plays. In this case, I was able to paint both Randy and the deputy as victims of Steve's machinations.

Effective communication and establishing a good, working rapport with your client can only help your case. Besides helping to manage expectations there are, as in Randy's case, helpful details that may never come to light without a good rapport and open line of communication. And details, the little pictures, are what fill in the big picture.

Now may be a good time to go slightly off topic. We'll get back to objections and foundations in a minute. You've got the message of the importance of details hammered into you, especially when laying foundations, but which details are important? Some are obvious, as in jurisdiction for a prosecutor. Some may be obvious to you, but not your client, as in Randy's case. It's part of trial preparation to effectively prioritize your details. You can do it witness-by-witness or issue-by-issue, whatever works for you. But at some point you will need to cross-reference them, so to speak, with all the moving parts. What do I mean?

A "trial notebook," for example. It's not enough to have the reports or interviews in order. What I like to do (and many experienced trial attorneys too, for that matter) is make an overall trial notebook with all of the discovery, reports, etc., in order, preferably Bate stamped, and then make separate notebooks that cross-reference the materials. Each witness (if they are an important witness, at least—less important witnesses can be combined into one notebook) I put into a separate notebook, and every piece of discovery that relates to that witness (e.g., reports, interviews, transcripts, photos) are in that notebook, tabbed and labeled. I've outlined each one or made notes, and in my notes referenced the others. There should be a table of contents as well. When that witness testifies, I have his or her notebook in front of me.

If time or resources don't allow, then one notebook with separate sections for each witness and sub-tabs/labels also works. It not only helps to organize your case and, therefore, your presentation, but helps to prioritize your witnesses and evidence. It also makes it easier to prepare, as you can just pull that notebook or tabbed section to prep, go over before trial and, when in trial, right before the witness testifies. It helps keeps the counsel table less cluttered too. The process also allows me to better focus on the details of each witness and piece of evidence, and the connections between different witnesses and evidence.

What does this have to do with "the heat of battle?" Isn't this better for the preparation section? Maybe you're beginning to get it—a trial is fluid. While there are different stages, they all intersect. How can you give a good presentation, lay the foundation smoothly, seamlessly, to impeach a witness or admit (eventually) a piece of evidence if you're a disorganized mess? Prioritizing evidence and arguments, reassessing and readjusting, objections, strategizing—it's all intertwined. The more organized, the better and more smoothly they will complement each other. There is a myriad of hearsay objections. I've gone over several as examples to emphasize their connection to the real objection to hearsay evidence, or at least the one that must always be made in conjunction with a hearsay objection: lack of foundation.

C. Facts Not in Evidence. This objection usually comes in two forms. The first is when the other attorney is asking about a fact or facts that have not yet been in evidence and require a foundation that has not yet been established. Not so silly question: aren't all facts, at some point, not yet in evidence? So, wouldn't this objection seem to apply all the time, almost ad nauseum? In this scenario, what the objection really means is that the fact being asked about needs a foundation to be relevant, to be connected to what has already been said or admitted into evidence. The primary focus of this objection is foundational: "Hey, you're asking about something that doesn't seem to have a connection to what's been said or admitted," (i.e., you're assuming that fact has already been asked about, documented, etc.) but it hasn't. In this form, the objection is requiring a foundation of personal knowledge by the witness that he or she was actually there or actually heard or saw what it is the attorney is asking about. Most of the time the attorney is just skipping ahead, and it's the lack of chronological order that is creating the issue.

The second reason for this objection is a more practical one: The attorney is actually asking about something that, simply, has not been introduced yet. It could be a statement or observation. But the attorney is not asking the witness about the truth or the witness's knowledge of the fact; on the contrary, the attorney is assuming the fact to be true and is using that fact now as a foundation for the next question. When an attorney does this, he or she is, for all intents and purposes, testifying.

D. Vague and Ambiguous. This objection is exactly what it purports to be. General questions are foundational questions. But once into the nuts and bolts of a witness's testimony, the questions need to be specific. Even direct examination questions need to be specific. Questions that are vague, as to time like the time of day or time of year, especially when it can be an issue in a case or is necessary to put things in proper perspective, need to be concise. Questions about feelings, thoughts, even actions, again, need to be put in context, which means specific to time and place. When attorneys fail to do this, it can be merely sloppy work or intentionally being vague to interpret the answer as self-servingly as possible. Either way, such questions are ripe for objections.[31] The more precise the question, the less the answer can be misinterpreted, be it inadvertently or purposefully.

E. Misstates the Testimony of the Witness. This objection is more of an overt message to the jury than a real objection. It's basically telling your audience, "Hey, she never said that! The attorney's trying to trick you!" Unless it's blatant or the judge is copious when it comes to details, most judges overrule this objection: "The record speaks for itself." That being said, there are still times you'll want to interject and let the jury know that the other side is acting slimy. It could've been a simple mistake and, if it was, no harm, no foul. But if not, at least you've alerted the jury to opposing counsel's tactics. It also serves to telegraph

---

31 An example of vagueness, although not from trial: When asking my wife where something might be in the house, she has the habit of simply nodding her head in the direction the object may be and stating, "Over there." My usual retort: "My love, a whole half a house is 'over there!' Can you be a little more specific?"

to your witness to be alert and focus on the question, and more specifically, the word choice.

F. Relevance. You'll notice that my commentary on relevance objections is short because the threshold for what's a relevant question of a witness is incredibly low. Relevance objections usually go hand in hand with foundation. A question asking about or posing a fact that seems irrelevant at the time it's asked really means that the attorney hasn't laid a factual foundation why this fact is relevant. Again, although the threshold for evidence or testimony to be relevant is low, it's not nonexistent, and still requires both a foundation as to why it's now relevant or relevant at all. When objecting based on relevance, then, it's good form at times to first object based on foundation, then relevance. "Objection: foundation, relevance." You'd be surprised how many times the judge will either sustain the objection or at least just instruct the attorney to lay a foundation. If the relevance is tangential and the attorney has been beating a dead horse, the objection may just get sustained, period.[32]

G. Evidence Code 352. In California you'll often hear attorneys object, "352." California evidence code section 352 has a number of issues for a judge to consider in determining if a question is seeking not only relevant information but also admissible information. The ones often cited, and generically can be made in any jurisdiction, are the following:

✓ *More Prejudicial Than Probative*

Simply put, this objection is stating that although the fact/testimony sought is relevant, it's highly inflammatory and would prejudice the jury against the side making the objection. You might be asking, then, so what? Too bad for the other side.

As an advocate in an adversarial system, that makes sense. But the judge deciding on the objection is tasked with

---

32 Be on guard for opinion testimony where it's really being offered to pander to emotion or ingratiate the witness to the jury. Opinion evidence is routinely sought and let in, but for the most part, it shouldn't be. Estimates of time, distance, etc., are valid opinion evidence. Feelings of fear, anger, frustration, depression may be relevant to explain actions or to assess damages, or as elements in a crime, but they're not relevant just to elicit humanistic responses for the sake of humanistic responses. Yet judges routinely let them in.

determining whether the probative value of the testimony or evidence is outweighed by its prejudicial effect. Remember, relevance is a very low threshold, so facts that are barely consequential may be relevant, but does their inflammatory character outweigh that relevance? That's the "balancing act" a judge needs to weigh when deciding on that objection.

Most facts or evidence that are prejudicial or inflammatory are usually the subject of motions *in limine*, or pre-trial motions, and thus their admissibility has been decided before the witness or evidence ever comes before a jury. For those issues that are not easily foreseen before trial, this objection should be in your pocket.

✓ *Cumulative*

"Judge, we've already basically heard or seen this before. Do we need more of this?" Cumulative means exactly what it sounds like—we're repeating the same evidence in different clothing and wasting time. Been there, done that. Do we need to ask that same set of questions for every witness or put on a third or fourth witness to say exactly what the first two said? Since most judges hate to waste time, this objection rings true to them.

H. Argumentative. I saved this objection for last because it is widely misunderstood. Though it makes good Hollywood, there is not a "badgering the witness" objection. "Argumentative" really means belittling the witness or not allowing the witness to answer the question. Many times, it's just the phrasing of the question that judges will jump on. It should be fair game on cross-examination to give a rundown of a witness's previous testimony to sum up his or her story, chronology, etc. But begin that question with, "So, is it your testimony that . . ." and you'll more times than not spark an objection that a judge will sustain. If it sounds confrontational, it probably is, and many judges will instinctively sustain an argumentative objection toward a confrontational question. Adding to that, it's been my experience that the more sympathetic a witness has come across, the more likely an argumentative objection will be sustained if the attorney seems confrontational.

There *are* certain "matchups," however, that are naturally confrontational and therefore will be given more latitude by a judge. For example, when a defendant in a criminal prosecution takes the stand, the word "sustained" to an argumentative objection simply never passes a judge's lips. They've waived their Fifth Amendment protections and, with that, seemingly any other protection the rules of evidence allow. To further complicate things, when his or her attorney objects "argumentative" and it's overruled, that sends a strong message to a jury—intentionally or not—that their client's in trouble. The same is true of a plaintiff in a civil case. So, if you're client is on the stand, be sparing with this objection. The best course of action is to prepare them well enough to hold their own. If opposing counsel is being confrontational long enough, he begins to look like a bully, and that never goes over well.

In general, objections are necessary tools of the trade, but like everything else in a trial, they must be weighed as to their utility before engaging the judge. There may be times when an attorney objects just to break up opposing counsel's rhythm or progress, or to give her witness a break. Those objections may be completely justified. But hearing a judge say too many times "Overruled" takes a toll. It can negatively impact the attorney's credibility and therefore her entire presentation. In essence, you need to pick your battles, even small skirmishes that occur in a split second, like when to make an objection. You should train your mind to ask yourself in literally a tenth of a second, "Is it worth it?" Too many objections, especially if you're being overruled, can destroy your credibility. On the other hand, if the judge and you seem to be on the same page, or if opposing counsel can't seem to ask a cogent question, it may be worth objecting, and objecting, and objecting. It's like constantly feeling the wind direction and deciding whether to tack or hold steady. It's a split-second decision that comes more easily with experience because it's one of the many factors to consider when navigating your case through trial.

IN THE HEAT OF BATTLE
Compass Points

. . .

Objections and Foundation
A. **Speculation**
B. **Foundation**
   • Hearsay—the truth of the matter asserted (within the statement)
      ✓ *Business Records and Documentation*
      ✓ *State of Mind/Future Actions Explained*
      ✓ *Bias*
      ✓ *Prior Inconsistent Statement*
C. **Facts Not in Evidence (there goes that foundation objection again!)**
D. **Vague and Ambiguous**
E. **Misstates the Testimony of the Witness**
F. **Relevance**
G. **California Evidence Code 352**
   • More prejudicial than probative
   • Cumulative
H. **Argumentative**

CHAPTER FIVE

PREPARING THE WITNESS

It is better to keep your mouth closed and let people think you are a fool than to open it and remove all doubt.

—MARK TWAIN

Unless all the evidence is stipulated to, every trial has witnesses: victims, defendants or moving parties to the action, percipient witnesses to the event, witnesses who lay a foundation for records, documents, or other items of evidence, expert witnesses. Depending on the kind of case it is and the complexity of the facts, the trial may include all of the above, or some, but *at least one*. Those witnesses need to be examined. If it's your witness, that means direct examination. If it's the other side's witness, that means cross-examination. Some attorneys think (and, unfortunately, put this misconception into practice) that direct examination is simply throwing your witness on the stand and asking some basic questions.

Wrong.

Some attorneys think that cross-examination means always confronting the witness, proverbially (or sometimes, literally) getting in the witness's face, bullying the witness, or keeping the opposing witness on the stand for as long as possible to wear him or her down and thus trip them up.

Equally wrong.

To use a baseball analogy, when I was a small kid, Tom Seaver was my favorite pitcher. Seaver had come up with the NY Mets and, together with Nolan Ryan, helped drive the team to win the 1969 World Series. Both had strong, hard fastballs. Nolan Ryan became legendary for his fastball; he was throwing over 90 mph long after the 1969 "Miracle Mets," even after the age of 40! Seaver, by the mid-1970s, had lost some edge on his fastball. So he expanded. Adapted. He developed a hard slider, a great curveball, and a solid changeup. And he stayed pitching for years, ultimately becoming a Hall of Famer. Sure, Nolan Ryan was also a great pitcher, and also an eventual Hall of Famer, but, in reality, there was only one Nolan Ryan. No one before or since has ever been able to reproduce his longevity and consistency. Had Ryan lost some speed on the fastball, he would have had to adapt, like his former teammate, or retire. Tom Seaver, on the other hand, stayed great because he had more than one great pitch in his pocket.

I tell younger, less experienced attorneys and clients that there was only one Nolan Ryan, and it ain't me. You can consistently win cases over the years if your strategy and approach can adapt to the case at hand and the witness on the stand. In my clinic during my last year of law school, one of my supervisors told me, "The best cross-exams are the ones where you pick their pocket, and they thank you afterward." That's a curveball, a changeup, but *not* a fastball.

Yes, I'd rather be a Tom Seaver.[33]

Prepping a Witness for Direct Examination

Different attorneys have different styles for preparing a witness for direct examination. Unless it's an expert witness, I usually do not prepare a witness, at least not by myself. But, if the attorney is preparing the witness, as alluded to in the last sentence, she should never do that by herself. Even if the witness is being recorded (which must be with

---

33 I really can't stress it enough. An attorney that can't change his approach depending on the witness and posture of the case is like the old joke about the clock that's broken. Sure, it's spot-on . . . twice a day! Don't be like that clock.

the witness's permission, unless the recording is being made by law enforcement to further the investigation of a crime[34]), if the witness testifies to something different than what he told the attorney, the only person that can impeach the witness or lay a proper foundation for the recording is the attorney. She then becomes a witness in the very trial in which she is an advocate, creating a real conflict of interest and credibility issue. And while there is case law that allows an attorney, even as an advocate to the proceeding, to testify in the proceeding, it looks ridiculous, unprofessional, and sloppy.

The better and right way to prep a witness (who is not your client) is with a third party present. Then, if anything goes awry, that third party can testify to what was said or lay the foundation for the recording, the one where the witness has agreed to being recorded.

In preparing a witness who is not your client, realize that anything said in that conversation or preparation, regardless of whether it was recorded, is fair game for discovery and can be examined at trial. So make sure that first, middle, and last, you let the witness know that he or she needs to be honest. If they don't remember something, unless something refreshes their memory (and you can certainly try) saying, "I don't remember" is not only the safest answer, it's also the honest answer.

My preparation for witnesses, a part of which I also use for clients (and much more, which we'll get into), is basic but works to make the person a much more relaxed and effective witness.

The first part of the preparation consists of two main parts, split into three subparts each.

Part I: General Demeanor and Method

Most witnesses, even experienced ones, are nervous when they take the stand. I've had nearly 200 jury trials, have spoken publicly to large and

---

34 I've seen family court attorneys advise clients to clandestinely record arguments or conversations with spouses to help further their arguments in family court, be it over child custody, child support, alimony, or the estate. In California, at least, that's a felony! There is no exception for the purpose of getting one up on a spouse during a messy divorce.

small audiences alike for almost 30 years, and I still get nervous every time I stand up to speak. It's only natural. Once I begin, most (but not all) of the butterflies go away. In the heat of the battle, well, let's just say there's no room for butterflies on a battlefield.

Rule of thumb in preparing witnesses and in life: *The more emotional and personal a subject or situation is for a person, the less that person will effectively communicate.* People can act calm, cool, and collected when disagreeing with a stranger or a colleague. But we all know from experience that the closer the relationship, the more easily our emotional buttons can be pushed. As I tell clients, *when the emotions kick in, the communications skills kick out.* Witnesses are no exception. The more personal the testimony, the more this applies (with victims and clients, the rule applies exponentially).

Being an effective communicator, be it a witness or an attorney, does not mean being completely dispassionate. Robotic testimony from witnesses or monotone presentations from an attorney never go over well. Witnesses and attorneys are human and need to show it. But the passion needs to be controlled. Unbridled emotions do not make for effective communication.

So, knowing that most witnesses will be nervous and prone to being influenced by their emotions (and the less experienced a person is at testifying, the more nervous), I start by giving them some easy dos and don'ts.

A. *Listen to the Whole Question.* Sounds easy enough, right? But it never happens, especially with an emotionally charged or nervous witness. We live in a very impatient society. Whether it's ordering items to be delivered the same day or, G-d forbid, two-day delivery, we've grown more and more impatient. The advent of texts, Snapchats, and quick sound bites becoming how we view the world, a society where research really means for most people five or ten minutes on a network browser (and I'm being generous), taking our time in conversations is a thing of the past. So I need to remind witnesses we're not in a rush. A good examination is the goal; it's not necessarily a quick one. Take your time. *Do not* interrupt the attorney with an answer, even if the question seems to be a no-brainer. And *do not* finish the question for the attorney, "Oh you mean [this]?" It doesn't serve the witness well, nor the attorney. For example, many times the attorney may ask a compound question, or be thinking out loud and in a stream of consciousness ask several thoughts in one question. Like a runaway train that does ultimately have a destination but is out of control getting there, the attorney may know what he's thinking, but the witness may not, which can lead to erroneous answers or, worse, open cans of worms. So drum into your witness to listen to the whole question. Practically speaking, if your witness is testifying on cross-examination, it gives you time to object. If it's direct examination, interrupting your question could negatively impact your credibility in front of the jury (Who's running the show, you or the witness?). It could also negatively impact the witness's credibility. By interrupting, she will look too eager to testify on behalf of your client. Sure, it may be your witness, and therefore she's testifying to help your case. But the jury still needs to at least perceive her as not only honest, but impartial too. Most people instinctively believe that honesty and impartiality go hand in hand. The more unbiased a witness comes across, the less of an agenda she will seem to have, and the more honest and sincere she will seem to the jury. "Just be a sponge," I tell my witnesses. "Soak up the question."

B. Pause. Probably the most important advice you can give a witness is to pause before answering a question. Not a long time, maybe one or two seconds at most.[35] Long enough to gather her thoughts. Witnesses should not have knee-jerk responses or react on the witness stand. They should be thinking. By pausing, she has time to stop and think. But again, no more than one or two seconds. Longer than that, and the jury or judge may grow impatient. They may even think the witness is trying to fabricate something on the spot.

---

35 Years ago, I had a client to whom I gave this preparation before his internal affairs interview. I didn't at the time mention that the pause period should be no more than one or two seconds. He obviously listened to my prep and took my advice to heart: The first three questions, he must have paused nearly two or three minutes between each question! We took a break, and his sergeant called me into the hallway. "Mike, I don't think he's lying. We just started and these are basic questions. But it's been almost ten minutes and we're just on question three!" I took the client aside, and both thanked him for listening to my preparation so well but added that I should have explained that when I said pause, I meant only one or two seconds at most! He thanked me, and said he'd go a little quicker. He did.

Pausing also slows things down. My general rule for all witnesses, and I've never seen its exception: the slower the examination, the better for the witness. My personal style is to vary my cross-examinations, but during many, if not most, there will be large or small parts where I'll launch into a rapid-fire cross-exam. It's my personal style. I naturally speak very quickly, think quickly, and know my facts, the sum total of which lends itself to rapid-fire cross-examinations. It's exciting for the jury to watch and hear because it's fast paced. It builds credibility for the attorney because you can't conduct a rapid-fire examination unless you know your facts cold and are in control. And it turns the witness into a puppet. The attorney then becomes the show, the center of attention, and can tell her client's story, or a piece of it, through an adverse witness. And for the witness, it's more than uncomfortable.

But if the witness is listening to the whole question and pausing, that can never occur. The rhythm of the examination is in the witness's control, not the attorney's control. It will help to relax the witness and empower them.

C. During That Pause Period, Think First, Speak Second.

Most people do not think before they speak, at least not in daily conversations. Communications would take much longer, and who has that kind of time?

The witness does.

I tell witnesses that not only do they have the time to listen to the entire question, pause, and then think before answering, but it's imperative. It's also their right. Their words are being scrutinized as they're saying them and will be further scrutinized as the case goes on, in comparison to other witnesses and other evidence. It will then be rehashed and scrutinized again in the closing argument and jury deliberation. So it's vital to articulate the answer as clearly and lucidly as possible. Listening to the whole question and pausing, then thinking, "What's the best way I can put this," *before answering* gives the witness the presence of mind to effectively communicate their answer.

Part II: Memory

Next comes memory. I tell potential witnesses that I want them to look at memory as a series of photographs spread across a table. In the middle of each photo, it's crystal clear,[36] toward the edge it's blurry, and in between the photos it's blank. I emphasize in my prep: That's how "you" should answer questions. If you know something 100%, then say it 100%. Be concrete. But just be honest with yourself how well you really know something. Most times we know what we didn't say or didn't do, but what we did say or do, if at the time it didn't seem significant, it might not be so memorable. A general rule of human behavior: Most people remember things that at the time it occurred seemed important or significant. The issue is that a lot of life becomes significant only after the fact, which can be days, weeks, or even months later (Try years!). But if it wasn't significant at the time the event itself occurred, then it may not be part of a person's memory. Conversely, most of us are, at least somewhat, creatures of habit. We have a very specific way of speaking, have phrases we like to commonly use, and know there are certain things that, even on our worst days, we would never do or say. So it's usually easier to confidently deny doing or saying something than to affirmatively remember doing or saying something. The key is to tell the witness to just be honest with herself about how well (or not) she remembers something.

You may have guessed the next line of preparation for the potential witness by the above discussion: I prepare the witness by telling them that if they really don't know the answer to a question, then that's their answer! *Do not* take an educated guess or try to fill in the blank to be helpful. If you don't know or don't remember, then you don't know or remember. That's it.

What about "refreshing recollection?" Well, that may work, but again, there's a caveat. I tell witnesses that, if after answering that they don't know or don't recall something and the next question is "Well, would [watching the video again] [reading the report] [reading a transcript of your prior testimony] help refresh your recollection?" The witness should never answer "Yes."

Why not?

Because how do they know that item will actually refresh their recollection until specifically confronted with it? The correct answer to

---

36 You can tell I'm old school, from the era of 35mm film. In today's world, with digital technology, the entire photo is pretty close to crystal clear, not just the middle!

that question is: "maybe." "Possibly." *Then*, after viewing, reviewing, or listening to the item that purports to refresh the witness's recollection, she can honestly answer either "Yes, it did" or "No, it didn't." And if it didn't, then time to move on. The witness doesn't know the answer to the question or recall the fact or incident.

Finally, what if the witness does recall part of the event or incident, but just not all of it? He has a partial memory, but not a complete memory. I tell witnesses to simply testify that way, to be very specific about what he does and does not remember—everyday phrases like "I'm not 100% sure" or "I could be wrong," "Don't quote me on that," "I half remember it this way" or "I vaguely remember"—whatever qualifier is appropriate that the witness feels comfortable with, in his own words, to articulate that the witness does not have a complete or full memory, is how the witness should answer the question. The main goal is credibility, which means honesty and accuracy, even if the accuracy is an admission to not having a complete picture.

Part III: Prepping Your Client for Testifying

All of the mentioned general preparation for witnesses applies to preparing your client as well, with two extra considerations: (1) Your client will be that much more stressed, that much more nervous because, unlike any other witness, your client has her future riding on her testimony. (2) The case is about your client, so if he or she does well it can bolster a good case or save a floundering case, but if he or she implodes, regardless of how well the case was going until that point, you're done and so is your client.

Those that claim that a witness is completely neutral and has no stake in the matter are either naïve, simply wrong, or lying. *Every* witness has a stake in his or her testimony. No one wants to come across as a liar or unbelievable in front of other people, be they twelve strangers or their family and friends. Every human being, even sociopaths and pathological liars want to be believed. Some witnesses will exaggerate or minimize their testimony just to make themselves look better, even though they are not a party to the action. Being questioned and cross-examined can be stressful for anyone.

When it comes to your client, multiply that natural discomfort and that stake in her testimony exponentially. Besides the natural tendency to want to be liked or at least believed, your client literally has her future riding on her testimony. If it's a civil case and you're the plaintiff attorney, or a criminal case and you're the prosecutor, she is hoping for remuneration for whatever wrong she feels she suffered, or vindication and justice if she is a victim of a crime. As a defense attorney in a criminal matter, her freedom is literally on the line. I have a general rule I tell my clients: Regardless of how well a trial may seem to be going, all bets are off when your client takes the stand. If the jury likes your client, that feeling can translate into empathy and winning over a juror to your side. But the opposite is true as well. If your client will alienate the jury, be disliked, or be unbelievable, your case is now over.

So, how do you prepare your client? And how much? Too much preparation and it looks rehearsed. Too little, and they are unprepared for cross-examination. It's a fine line. Much of the equation depends on your client's natural abilities. Appearance, as shallow as it sounds, does make a difference. No one can help their natural looks. But dressing appropriately, body language—those tangibles are within your control. Your client should dress in a way that telegraphs to the jury that she knows how important this is. She's not going to a wedding or a bar, so taste, decorum, and respect for the forum should dictate how she is presented throughout the entire process, and especially when she testifies. This may sound basic, but as attorneys we live and breathe in the professional world (and even then, I've seen many an attorney dress inappropriately for trial). You need to make sure you instruct your client how to dress. Do not assume they know appropriate dress codes for court, be it a judge alone or a jury. Trials are your world, not theirs.

Some attorneys prepare their clients by sequestering them for eight hours and cross-examining them. If it works for them, great. That's not my approach. I have conversations and meetings with my client about the case and, specifically, their story, their testimony. I give them my thoughts, and how I would phrase things, how I look at things. It's a conversation. And then another. And another. Throughout the pending litigation, we meet and discuss their case. On the phone too. When we get closer to trial, those conversations grow longer and become peppered, little by little, with cross-exam type questions and some incredulity. We flow in and out of character and discuss it. Again, I also phrase things and think out loud.

I do all of this so that my way of articulating facts or looking at the case becomes part of my client's way of articulating as well. It's every attorney's dream to be able to testify for his client, like one of those Disney movies where the parent and kid switch bodies. By slowly, incrementally, and informally discussing the case, their story, their testimony, and how I view it and articulate it, almost by osmosis they begin to see and speak it "my way" as well. I haven't changed any facts, but I've influenced how my client thinks about and presents those facts. By the time we get to mock examinations, both direct and cross-examination, it's natural. Even then, I'll never go more than three hours in a "session." Too long a session, and everyone gets worn out. Too many long, intense sessions, and you may lose the raw emotion—it comes out in "practice," and not when it counts. There's a balance. Bottom line: It needs to be, and remain, real.

I also tell my client, more than once, that although it will be uncomfortable, they need to be themselves. Yes, it's unnerving. Yes, it's embarrassing. But if they put on a face, try to hide their emotions too much (as opposed to just being in control of their emotions), there'll be something about them that won't seem quite right. Off. Disingenuous. The jury will sense it but, not knowing your client personally, will think your client is being less than honest in what they're saying, not in how they're saying it. Game over.

"Be yourself; everyone else is already taken."
—OSCAR WILDE

Years ago, I had an arbitration case that really hit that point home. My client "Jim," a detective for a police agency, had been accused by his estranged stepdaughter of molesting her between the ages of fifteen and eighteen. She made the allegations after a messy divorce when she was twenty-three years old, at least five years after the "youngest" of the allegations had allegedly happened. Besides vehemently denying the claims, he was emotionally devastated. He had raised her as his own daughter since she was two years old.

He agreed to take a polygraph exam but, during the pre-exam questions, became too emotional to continue. The prosecutor's office declined to file the case due to the age of the accusations. He went through an internal affairs investigation, and the recommendation was for termination; the chief believed the accusations. We attended a Skelly meeting with his chief where, while angrily denying the allegations, he broke down crying. He'd lost twenty pounds already; he was a wreck.

The chief didn't believe him. He was terminated.

In the intervening year from his termination until his arbitration hearing, we prepared for his testimony. We met once, twice, probably about a dozen times over coffee, sometimes at my office. We talked about the case and his relationship with his stepdaughter. Sure, we'd met and spoken before. But now he'd be testifying. Every time we went over the allegations, he got emotional. He'd turn red, cry. He really couldn't discuss the accusations without a mixture of anger and hurt.

Jim was a former Marine who, after an honorable discharge, got a job as a meat-packer to pay the bills. He then re-enlisted in the National Guard reservists. He wasn't a wimp; he was tough and had lived with hardship most of his life. But this was different—this was an accusation that went to the very core of who he was: a kind, honest, good man.

The hearing began well. I cross-examined his stepdaughter and not only caught her in more than a few notable discrepancies, but in some obviously unbelievable facts as well. As I stated before, the devil in litigation is in the details. Many a lie is unraveled when going into detail after detail. By the time her testimony was through, I felt I'd done a good job of discrediting her.

Her brother, who the city called to testify to support her story was equally incredible when put to the test and contradicted some of her narratives. It's a somewhat common occurrence in cases—to be witness blind. Many attorneys automatically empathize with either their client, or (if a prosecutor or city attorney/county counsel in an administrative matter) the alleged victim or police chief and never bother to objectively scrutinize the witness's story or potential testimony. The city attorney made the same mistake here. By the time she had finished with her case-in-chief, if Jim could simply hold his own, I thought we had a real shot at winning the arbitration.

Jim's direct examination went well enough. It lasted about an hour and a half, and he seemed to answer just fine, but something was off.

Then came cross-examination. Again, although he seemed to be answering OK, I could sense something off. In almost two hours of testimony, he hadn't cried once. Not even glassy-eyed. We broke for lunch, and Jim and I got in his car to grab a coffee for me and a bite for him. I started the conversation.

"Jim," I looked over at him, "you nervous?"

"I have to admit yeah, a little."

"I gotta ask you—are you putting on a face for the arbitrator?"

He shrugged, and his expression turned a little sheepish. "Yeah, I don't want her to see me cry."

"WHAT?!" I yelled (I actually did!) "You went for the polygraph, and you turned red and cried. We went for the IA interview, and you turned red, broke down, and cried. We sat with your chief for the Skelly meeting, and you turned red and cried! Every time we've dealt with this you've gotten emotional! And now," I paused, to let it sink in, "now, in front of the arbitrator who met you only two days ago, you put on a John Wayne face?" I leaned over slightly. "I know you're putting on a face because I *know* you! But she doesn't know you! This is a credibility contest, and you're being fake! I'm not telling you to cry, but I *am* telling you that you better start being yourself! If you feel emotions, don't hold back. Be *you*!"

We went back after lunch, and the city attorney started cross-examining him on a child custody declaration that he admittedly had fudged at the beginning of the divorce a few years prior to get back at his ex-wife. She was doing a good job, attacking his credibility on that issue to spill it over into our case. But in doing a good job, she became overconfident and then arrogant. She left that topic and began asking about the specific allegations. Jim denied one after the other. I could see his blood beginning to boil. Then came the question, posed mockingly, almost coquettishly.

"You've denied the allegation about the forcible oral copulation on the ride-along and at your house, and the other allegations, but you sat here and saw and heard her testify . . . why would she lie?"

The city attorney was smirking, but not for long. Jim blew a gasket. His face turned as red as a fire truck. His eyes welled up. Before I could even think of objecting to speculation, he yelled, almost screamed: "I DON'T KNOW WHY SHE'S LYING! I raised her since she was two! She's my daughter! I thought I knew her! My whole world turned upside down a year and a half ago! I can't sleep, I can't eat. I don't know what's reality and what's not! She's my daughter! She's my daughter!" He put his face in his hands and sobbed.

We paused for a couple of minutes. When we resumed, the city attorney tried to regroup. She asked him about statements from his internal affairs interview. "If it's in there (referring to the transcript), I said it!" was all Jim could answer back. She asked questions about his polygraph answers. "If it's in there, I said it." Jim's face beet red. Over and over again. We closed our case with a couple of character witnesses. Three months later, the arbitrator ordered the police department to give Jim his job back.

I'll never forget that case or the lesson learned. Your client has really one opportunity to tell his story, one opportunity to connect with your audience, be it a jury, judge, or arbitrator. It has to be *real*.

Skewing

While this section could easily appear in one of the next couple of chapters on direct and cross-examinations, I always go over this less-than-ethical tactic with witnesses to help them avoid the hidden land mines the tactic is meant to create.

Skewing is when an attorney inserts a fact into a question that, by outward appearances, is not really the essence or primary fact the question is trying to elicit. It can almost appear innocuous. But it's not.

At its best and most insidious, skewing is asking a question that, while not compound, borders on it in such a way as to not be objectionable, but allows the attorney—who has now elicited a "yes" or "no" answer—to pick which fact within the question the witness actually agreed or disagreed to. It's very much a game of semantics, but hidden semantics. And it works. It "skews" the answer to the interpretation that the examiner wants. What makes it unethical to many attorneys? When a question has more than one fact within it or by the way the question is worded, it's almost impossible for the witness to answer the question fairly, it's skewing.

Simple examples I give potential witnesses:

Fact pattern:

Your client is being sued for a wrongful death after hitting and killing a pedestrian who was in the street but not in a crosswalk. One of the issues is the speed at which your client's car was going both at the point of impact and one thousand feet before. The CHP MAIT report cannot estimate the speed accurately, so it will be (and probably would've been, anyway) a battle of accident reconstruction experts on both sides, and percipient witnesses. If your client was speeding, then he was negligent, and the case against him is that much stronger. You prepare your client for testifying. It was a traumatic experience, and you make sure you prepare him for the emotions that will flow. You need to also prepare him for skewing.

"Mr. Smith, good afternoon.

"Good afternoon, ma'am."

"You testified this morning that right before this accident occurred where you hit and killed my client's son, you were on your way to work?"

"Yes, that's right."

"Drive that same route all the time, correct?"

"Almost every day."

"Know it pretty well, then?"

"I'm still careful."

"Like the back of your hand?"

"I know it pretty well."

"So, you left your house around six thirty in the morning?"

"About that time."

"Usual time?"

"Yeah."

"Your normal routine?"

"Normally."

"And so you leave your house, back out of the driveway, and head south on Roundtree, your street?"

"I usually back out and go right. If that's south, OK."

"Go down Roundtree, make a left onto First Street?"

"There's a stop sign there—"

"Fair enough. First, you stop at the stop sign, right?"

"Yes."

"Then you make a right onto First Street, go all the way down, and make another right onto Eastvale?"

"Yes."

"And Eastvale takes you fast to Broadway, where the accident happened when you killed my client's son?"

"It was an accident—he wasn't in a crosswalk."

"Right. But it happened on Broadway?"

"Yes."

"So, just so I have your path down, let's go back. You pull out of your driveway around 6:30 a.m., go south, which is right, down your street, to First Street. You make sure you stop at the stop sign before making a quick right onto First Street where you go all the way down to Eastvale, then fast to Broadway, quick right on Broadway, and it's there that you hit my client's son who was in the street but not in a crosswalk. Is that accurate?"

"Yes."

In the last question, I used the words "quick" and "fast" in summing up the witness's actions. If said a bit quickly, it would have the dual effect of "feeling" quick or urgent. Now the chronology was accurate. And the last phrase in the summation, regarding the collision being an accident because the decedent was where he was not supposed to be, sounded safe to the witness. *But* . . . once the witness answered yes to that whole set of facts, the witness admitted and acknowledged that he was driving "fast" and "quickly" before striking the decedent.

Skewing.

In preparing your client or any witness, you need to alert and coach him to be aware and ready for such questions. If this were my client, I'd make sure he was focused on listening to the specific word choices of the opposing counsel and prime him to listen for words such as "quick," "speed," "race," "fast," etc., within the body of the questions. It's fair game to object if opposing counsel has "misstated the witness's prior testimony." But, if you've prepared your witness well, he (if he has the presence of mind and has incorporated your witness prep) can also simply correct the examiner.

"I wasn't driving fast, counsel."

"It's not a quick right. I stopped and then made a normal right-hand turn."

Preparing your client to correct the record, as opposed to objecting and doing it for him, is more powerful as well.

PREPARING THE WITNESS
Compass Points

• • •

A. Prepping a Witness for Direct Examination
- General Demeanor and Method
  - ✓ *Listen to the whole question.*
  - ✓ *Pause*
  - ✓ *Think first, speak second.*
- Memory
  - ✓ *If you know it 100%, be concrete.*
    - a) Be honest with yourself about how well you know something.
    - b) It is usually safer to be sure of denials.
  - ✓ *If you don't know the answer, then that's your answer.*
    - a) Don't take a guess or an "educated" guess.
    - b) Don't fill in the blank to be helpful.
  - ✓ *If you have a partial or incomplete memory, then testify that way.*
    - a) "I could be wrong . . ."
    - b) "Don't quote me on that . . ."
    - c) "I vaguely remember . . ."

B. Preparing Your Client for Testifying
- Keep it real.
- Presentation means everything.
  - ✓ *Dress code*
  - ✓ *Body language*
  - ✓ *Eye contact—look at the examiner, not at the jury.*
- Be yourself.
- Practice with your client; *converse* with your client.
- Skewing
  - ✓ *Prepare your client for red-flag words or phrases.*
  - ✓ *Prepare your client to focus intently on the entire question.*

CHAPTER SIX

DIRECT AND CROSS-EXAMINATION

*Cross-examination is beyond any doubt the
greatest legal engine ever invented for
the discovery of truth.*

—JOHN HENRY WIGMORE

Direct Examination: A Misunderstood Art

There are really three ways to conduct a direct examination. The first is to ask your witness mostly leading questions to get what you want from him or her. If there are no objections (and there should be), you've managed to get out your facts while boring the jury into oblivion. Your witness becomes a puppet with no personality of his or her own, and no story to tell. As I stated—*boring!*[37]

---

37 There are nuances to expert witness testimony, and some necessity for leading questions. The same can be said of child witnesses. But most of those "necessary" leading questions are simply the need to lay a foundation. While foundational questions may be exceptions to the "boring the jury to death" trap, they're not complete exceptions. An attorney should not assume, therefore, that just because she or he has an expert on the stand, or a child, the door is now fully open for an hour of leading questions.

The second method is for the lawyer to ask constantly: "What happened next?" "And then what happened?" "And then what did you do?" If the witness is not an expert, or a child witness or any witness of limited understanding or capacity, in order to tell her or his story (which *is* what testimony is, after all) the jury needs to be interested and connect (i.e., it sincerely needs to be *her* or *his* story, and not the attorney's). Leading questions become the attorney's story. *That's* for cross-examination (which we will get into in the next section). Direct examination is the witness's story. Sure, "What happened next" and "Then what did you do" seem to solve this problem, but it gets boring and diminishes the witness's role, thereby diminishing her or his stature, credibility, and testimony. Yes, it's a fine line. Remember, a trial is chess. No move, which in trial means no witness or examination, is trivial or insignificant; some moves are just more significant than others. But like in chess, all moves, meaning all examinations, count.

The third method walks that fine line. Again, know your facts. Cold. The best presentation for direct examination is when it seems comfortable, almost relaxed. The less you need to rely on notes (and try your best to not be reading from a list of questions, not on direct or on cross-examination), the more the examination will feel natural and convey a sense of truth— yes, truth—to the jury. The perception many laypeople have is that people who are being honest don't need to constantly refer to notes or prepared questions. Once or twice, maybe. But certainly not the lawyer, and not with her own witness! She or he is supposed to know the case, the facts, everything. If you need to be reading from a script, for *your* witness, how much confidence and credibility are you really building with your audience? It screams of a lack of either preparation, care, or both.

So, again, begin with knowing your facts. Again, cold. Ask several foundational questions to establish how the witness is connected to the case. If it is a percipient witness to the events, establish them at the location, their knowledge of the parties he or she is testifying about, why he or she was there, their relationship to your client, the other party, the place, etc. When you're ready to go into what he or she *actually witnessed*, be it visually, audibly, or both, *let the witness tell the story*. The "what happened next," when you need to ask it, should many times be prefaced with a brief sentence of what the witness just testified to in order to put the next question in context and reiterate the last piece of testimony.

"So after you screamed for him to leave, and he refused, then what happened?"

"So after you screamed for him to leave, and he refused, did you call the police?"

"Why not?"

"You were too scared to call out to anyone . . . could you even talk at that point?"

"You were too scared to talk or even move . . . then what happened?"

When the attorney prefaces the question with all or part of the last answer, he or she becomes part of the drama, part of the story, without telling it herself. The jury needs to connect with your witness, while not completely leaving you out of the picture. That only happens if that fine line is walked. It also allows the lawyer to look sympathetic, even empathetic, which also connects the attorney to the jury through the witness.

The above is even more pronounced when your client testifies. As I already stated, I tell clients that regardless of how well a case is going, once the client takes the stand, all bets are off. If the jury likes or empathizes with the client, you can turn what had been a losing cause into a win. But if the jury disbelieves or dislikes the client, you can also be grabbing defeat from the jaws of victory. It's one of the main reasons in criminal cases that although my client has a right to testify, I routinely advise him or her not to testify. Even if your client is honest, too many things can go wrong. Most people are not confident public speakers. Add the stress of wily cross-examination, his or her entire future being at stake, and many times it's a recipe for disaster.

Another consideration when your client testifies is now *both* of you need to walk a fine line. If it looks too rehearsed, the jury won't buy it. You're done. Game over. If you don't prepare enough, your client will not only get destroyed on cross-examination, he or she also won't hit the home run pitches that they should on direct. Even the best public speakers don't do everything (and really not many things) completely off the cuff. I tell people that we rehearse to ourselves or with impromptu audiences constantly[38] (like I stated, many times out loud) by repeating phrases, pieces of the closing argument, questions. And some parts of examinations—for example, foundations for impeachment, evidence, beginnings of cross-exams—have been done so often that it becomes like hitting the replay button in your brain. And even *then*, we can muff it! There's no way, with all that pressure and lack of experience, for your client to hit a home run, even in direct, without preparation.

Again, for direct examination in general but even more so when it's your client, not too many, if any, notes. The jury expects you to know the case and especially your client's story. If you need notes, it will come across as detached and, therefore, impersonal. If the lawyer is detached and un-connected to her or his client, why should the jury connect? Remember, most jurors see a trial as a morality play. Which means the lawyer, pro-fessionally, calmly, still needs to evoke a feeling of injustice, that her or his client (or victim) has been wronged (or, if defending a civil case, is in the right). If the attorney doesn't know his client's case and story, then he didn't bother to prepare enough, which means he really didn't care.

Neither will the jury.

Cross-Examination: *Oliver Twist* vs. *Perry Mason*

Most laypeople have a perception of trials based on movies, television, and books. The stereotypical perception is that cross-examination *must* mirror a *Perry Mason* episode.[39] Perry Mason, the intelligent defense attorney who represented only innocent clients, never lost a case, (but one, actually) and, for the most part, won each case with a biting cross-examination of the true culprit whom he was able to break down on the witness stand each and every episode. With that as the typical juror's expectation (not to mention Sam Waterston in *Law and Order*),

---

38 Many times, my wife and kids act as my sounding boards, where I can "argue" my case or evidence. Sometimes it's a friend or interested colleague. Many times, I'm speaking out parts of a closing argument or questions for a witness in my car or on a walk. I also go over thoughts with my client, almost in the form of a pep talk, be it giving over thoughts for voir dire, closing, etc.

39 The popular courtroom drama series aired from 1957–1966 and became both a symbol and myth of effective cross-examination.

most attorneys walking to the podium or standing at the counsel table have a tough act to follow. But, as I noted before, most attorneys, just like most major league baseball pitchers, are not Nolan Ryan, at least not for every witness. Nor should they be. Different witnesses present different issues and considerations unique to who they are and what part they play in the trial. Therefore, they require different approaches.

Besides the cutting, confrontational approach of Perry Mason, there's another approach: "Oliver Twist." If you recall, in the Charles Dickens classic, Oliver Twist was an orphan who fell in with Fagin, a despicable adult leader of a group of child pickpockets in Victorian London, the legendary "Artful Dodger" being one of the most experienced and skilled among the group. The "Dodger" quickly taught the orphan-runaway Oliver street smarts and pickpocketing, and a friendship was formed. The key to their success was that they were children and came across as young, vulnerable, and, therefore, nonthreatening and "innocent" to their prospective victims. They'd bump into people, then apologize and beg for a donation or handout, eliciting merciful responses from the front, while the other picked the unassuming victim's pocket from behind. In fact, many times the poor, unsuspecting dupe of the tag-team thieves would even ask if there were anything else they (the dupe) could do for them (the thieves)!

In trial, picking the witness's pocket is usually safer and therefore more recommended than a confrontation (the 6th Amendment notwithstanding). Sure, there are times to confront the witness, but like I've stated, you need to pick those battles.

Picking the witness's pocket means getting the information or facts you need in a nonthreatening way or in a way that once you lead the witness to where you need him or her to be, they really have no choice but to answer how you want them to answer, or look the fool. It means strategizing, thinking about your cross-examination as a game of chess, with different moves meant to provoke different responses. But the most important aspect is to remain calm, poised, polite. Sometimes, almost apologetic. It disarms the witness, endears you to your audience. If the time does come when you need to be confrontational, not only will the witness not see it coming until it's too late, but you'll also have credibility with the jury, who will see the contrast and understand why you're now turning up the heat. In trials with multiple witnesses, it may be that you've been calm and polite for certain witnesses and then, *bam!* One witness incurs your "wrath" (which, in reality, is controlled righteous indignation). The jury will get it!

Remember, the most effective fastball is usually after you've thrown a hard slider, a couple of good changeups, and maybe a curveball.

Looping

"Looping" is a method of pocket picking. Looping is taking a fact that speaks to the heart of your cross-examination or, at times, your case, and looping that fact or issue into your cross-examination multiple times. Like the now-illegal method of inserting a frame or two of popcorn and Coca-Cola every tenth frame in a movie so that, at some point, people will subconsciously think of popcorn and soda enough to get up and make the purchase. Inserting the fact subtly into your cross-examination, using synonyms and like phrases, subliminally influences your listener. An example of looping:

Let's say your client is charged with armed robbery. Mrs. Smith, an 85-year-old alcoholic, was pushed down and her purse grabbed from her at 1:30 a.m. in front of Ralph's Liquors. She didn't get a good look at her assailant yet made an identification at an in-the-field show up. Her ID was not solid, and identity becomes an issue at trial. You're now cross-examining Officer Nelson, the first officer on scene investigating the robbery.

Your client wants you to ask Mrs. Smith how she could see his face if it was 1:30 a.m. and dark. Of course, if you ask her that, she'll claim she did. So instead, you use Officer Nelson to impeach Mrs. Smith's identification . . .

"Officer Nelson, good morning."

"Good morning."

"You testified yesterday that you were called to the front of Ralph's Liquors last August 25 at about 1:30 a.m.?"

"Yes."

"You were dispatched to investigate a robbery?"

"Correct."

"Now, it was one thirty in the morning, right?"

"Yes."

"Ralph's had just closed?"

"I don't know."

"Well, when you arrived it was closed, right?"

"Yes, that's right."

"Now, in front of Ralph's, there's no streetlight, right?"

"I'm not sure."

"If I showed you a picture of the front of Ralph's Liquors, would that refresh your memory?"

"Sure."

"Showing you what's been marked as People's 2, for identification. Officer, is that a photo of the front of Ralph's Liquors?"

"Yeah."

"Any streetlights?"

"No."

"Refresh your memory that there were no streetlights on August 25 at 1:30 a.m. when you were dispatched to investigate a robbery call?"

"Yeah, there were no streetlights."

"And at 1:30 a.m., no traffic?"

"Not really, no."

"Early morning hours, right? Not many people out?"

"Right."

"Safe to say it was dark, right?"

"Yeah, but I could see OK."

"Well, when you parked you had your spotlight on, right?"

"Yeah."

"Because it was dark, right?"

"Yes."

"And when you got out of your car, you contacted a Mrs. Smith?"

"I did."

"She was standing on the sidewalk, kind of upset?"

"Yes."

"You used your flashlight to help see her face and the sidewalk where she described the robbery happened, right?"

"Yes."

"Because it was dark, no streetlights?"

"My spotlight worked pretty well."

"You weren't there when the robbery occurred, safe to say?"

"No, counsel, I wasn't."

"And neither was your spotlight, again, fair to say?"

"Fair to say."

"Even with the spotlight, you still had to use your flashlight at times?"

"Yes."

Etc.

You get the picture.

Inserting "It was dark," or "No streetlights," or "You had your flashlight out," every few questions hammers home the point not only intellectually, but emotionally. So in the closing argument when you need to impeach Mrs. Smith's testimony about her identification of your client, you've used Officer Nelson and the darkness, both intellectually and emotionally, to do it. Let alone to impeach her while she testifies. Looping can be used for any fact or issue—safety issues, time estimates, feelings (anger, frustration). And it works. Once inserted a few times, should the witness then decide to dispute that fact, you can then impeach them with all the times he or she agreed to that same fact, albeit maybe with a different phrase or word choice.[40]

The Kelly Thomas Murder Case

In July of 2011, I got a phone call, actually a series of them, from six officers of the Fullerton Police Department. They had been involved in a violent arrest about a week before, some of which was caught on a by-stander's cell phone video. It had gone viral, and the father of the suspect was on mainstream media, social media, you name it, demanding the officers be prosecuted. The suspect's name was Kelly Thomas, a 37-year-old homeless man. In resisting arrest, he had struggled for nearly five minutes with officers until, finally, he was handcuffed and controlled. He went into a coma and was pronounced brain dead about a week later. The coroner's report determined that "mechanical compression" (i.e., that too much weight was placed on him) constricted his breathing to such a degree that his brain did not get enough oxygen.

I was in the office when, one by one, the six officers, who had just been taken off work and placed on administrative leave, called in. I took the calls, had brief intake-oriented conversations to screen the calls,

---

40 Looping is a form of priming. Priming can and should also be used in *voir dire*, as we will discuss in the last chapter.

and decided that it'd be best to have a meeting with all six to let them know what to expect in what was fast becoming a national case and a statewide call for their heads.

The sixth officer, Jay Cicinelli, who'd later become my client, called last. He was a respected corporal, solid family man, and the next in line for promotion to sergeant. His captain, at trial, described him as one of their best. I remember the first five minutes.

Jay: "To be honest, I feel kinda dumb calling you and wasting your time. I didn't do anything wrong, certainly not criminal. I never needed a lawyer in my life and really don't think I need one now."

Me: "Well, not to burst your bubble, but you're not the first client to tell me that, and probably won't be the last."

Over the next week he called me a few times. I answered his questions, his wife's questions, even his dad's. We began to bond. Jay was the officer I "kept" as a client. So, when I met with all six officers, one order of business was to tell them that I was *not* giving them legal advice, just a rundown of what to expect, because we'd have to assign each of them to different attorneys outside our firm to avoid any conflict of interest.

About two months later, in September of 2011, Jay Cicinelli was charged with one count of involuntary manslaughter, and one count of felony battery under color of authority. One of his partners, Manny Ramos, was charged with second-degree murder.

Manny Ramos's attorney was John Barnett, a legendary defense attorney in Southern California. He was older than me, a big name. He'd been practicing for over twenty-five years and had a reputation for being the best. After trying a case with him, I can confidently say John is the best, the quintessential trial attorney. Although in the beginning of the case's investigative/workup process he seemed aloof, as we got into trial, his guard came down, and we began to work well together. Orange County was his home turf. The judges knew him and respected him. His client was charged with murder, although it was my client that was accused of "bludgeoning Kelly Thomas's face into oblivion."[41] So I let him take the lead when it seemed practical.

---

41 A quote from a local newspaper, covering the acquittal.

Why do I bring this up? Because you're never too old or experienced to learn from someone else. Trying a case with John Barnett and, even more, watching and listening to him became both educational and enjoyable. Our styles had similarities, but also differences. Watching him and actually trying a case with him helped me grow.

John is the picture of calm, cool, and poised. He is a great example of picking a pocket of a witness. When a witness begins to go offtrack, self-servingly not answering the question posed but instead begins to testify to his or her own agenda, the lawyer has several choices, as already described. Object. Tap dance. Or . . . do what John often does: simply talk to the witness. He smiles, puts his hand up, and says almost casually, "I know you want to talk about that. But we're not there yet. We'll get there, don't worry." Then he slides right back into his examination.

I saw him do that several times during the preliminary hearing when examining the pathologist. I loved it so much I incorporated it into my approach. When he repeated the style at trial, I had already decided to adopt it, varying it slightly to fit my personal style and that of the witness on the stand. I've used it ever since.

Like I stated above, my style was more Tom Seaver than Nolan Ryan. So copying John's style for that one point or approach with a difficult witness wasn't a 180-degree turnaround; it came naturally. I already had a reserved, even-tempered demeanor, calling out my passionate side when the right timing presented itself. This small but effective tactic was like adding a better changeup to my arsenal of pitches. Or maybe a different way of executing the changeup. And it works on two fronts:

- It presents to the jury that you're in control, and unruffled, building your credibility.
- It keeps you calm, poised, and levelheaded.

What am I getting at? Basically, that there are two schools of approach to cross-examination. They are not and should not be mutually exclusive. Unfortunately, many attorneys make that mistake. You can and should utilize both when you're able, like different pitches for different batters.

Your bottom line is to get out of that witness what you want from him or her. And to do it in a way that builds credibility with your jury. Looking and *being* in control does that. Which means picking your battles wisely. An overly aggressive attorney who knows only that overly aggressive approach on cross-exam looks like ... *an overly aggressive attorney who only knows that approach on cross-exam.* One pitch. That's it. And, after a while, it will tend to either alienate or bore a jury (or both), destroying that attorney's credibility. If you remain calm and poised, then when a witness does give you a reason to be aggressive, the jury will support it. So, when discussing cross-examination techniques, always keep this in mind like a mantra: "pick your battles."

Like I've said, in the Kelly Thomas case, though John and I had similar styles, our personas and execution were different. They turned out to complement each other.

Special Agent Jeff Smith[42]

When presented with a witness who seems very pleased with himself, the strategy I've employed over the years, and recommend, is instead of fighting with that ego, feed it. Like the starter for making good sourdough bread, egos like to be fed, and fed often. It's a form of picking that witness's pocket. Like the old phrase says, you catch more bees with honey than with vinegar.

Jeff Smith was a retired supervisor from the FBI flown in from Washington, DC to testify for the prosecution as a subject matter expert in law enforcement use of force. He had been with the bureau for nearly thirty years, had extensive training in FBI arrest and control tactics, as well as instructing agents in those tactics. He looked about mid-fifties, fit, clean-shaven, neat, blondish hair now turning gray. He wore an American flag tie. The only thing missing from the credentials he rattled off were an apple pie and actual experience as a street cop with certain street cop tools (i.e., a taser and collapsible asp). His skeletal report consisted mainly of his training and background, and a general opinion that the force was excessive. Although passing muster for state court (it wouldn't even be considered a first draft for a federal court Rule 26 report), it basically meant nothing to us. Our cross-exams, then, would depend on our knowledge of police tactics, the video evidence (which he really hadn't reviewed that closely), and "trial judo." John and I would

---

42 Not the real name.

have to see what he testified to on direct and, nearly on the fly, incorporate it into what we'd prepared for cross-exam.

We did.

Although that may sound like common practice, usually an expert provides some details in his or her report, giving the attorney more foundation going into cross-exam. Wilson had given us basically none.

General to Specific

Part of the picking the pocket approach is to lead the witness down a logical path, calmly, logically, with small, leading, common sense questions, many of which incorporate what they've already testified to, which, because familiar, lowers their guard. When dealing with a large ego, just add questions that seem to inflate that ego or at least acknowledge the witness's expertise. Step-by-step, the questions go from *more general to specific*, each one still incorporating something familiar, something of the last question or the several before it. They should be short, although they need not be monosyllabic. The point is to lull the witness into a false sense of security. By being calm, respectful, even deferential, the witness feels either you're fishing, lost, or just taking up time. But little by little, they're painting themselves into their own corner. You're just giving them the brush and the can of paint. By the time you hit them with the last one or two *specific* questions on that topic, it almost doesn't matter what their answer is. If they answer logically, you've won, and proven your point because that last question was the logical end to the trail you've led them down. If they refuse to answer logically, and instead get defensive, they'll not only look defensive they'll look like a fool as well. Arrogant witnesses usually opt for the fool's approach.

On direct examination, Smith had proven he had an ego. He described his position with the FBI as the equivalent of a one-star general in the Army. He opined that John Barnett's client, Manny Ramos, was excessive and out of control when he threatened Kelly Thomas with clenched fists to comply or he'd beat him up. Problem was, Manny Ramos had already used a similar tactic with Kelly Thomas about a year earlier, when he had threatened him with a baton if Thomas didn't comply. In that contact, it worked, and Thomas complied.

John could have simply asked Smith about the prior incident, and how Kelly Thomas finally complied. But that would have given Smith the ability to distinguish and contrast between the two, based on the details. Instead, utilizing the method I described above, John asked Smith general questions about tactics and human behavior—that if a tactic had worked in the past, wouldn't it be prudent, consistent with training and therefore reasonable, to employ it or a similar tactic again? And aren't officers trained that when something has worked in the past, to try that "tried and proven method" again before going to a different tactic or approach? Of course, the answers were yes. And isn't utilizing a trained upon tactic that has proven effective *reasonable*?

Again, yes.

John also asked questions about the reasonableness of using threats of force instead of resorting to force at the outset. Again, logical, general, common-sense questions. Start with command presence to gain compliance. Then commands themselves. Then threat of force, perhaps arrest. All the while reiterating the desire for the officer, based on his training, to try nonviolent methods first before having to "go hands on."

John then asked several hypotheticals, again, getting Smith to agree that officers are trained that a *threat* of less than lethal force can be very effective to deescalate a situation and gain compliance. He asked several more hypotheticals using different tools or tactics as examples: OC pepper spray, threat of baton strikes, even simply command presence. And again, the logical and intelligent responses had to be "yes," officers are trained to use the threat of such force to gain compliance, which means that threatening the use of force, in the right circumstances, is reasonable. Then John spoke to a particular incident, the one the year before, when Officer Ramos had used the threat of a baton strike to gain Kelly Thomas's compliance.

When questioning Smith about that incident, it became apparent, again, through the logical progression of questions, that it was also in Kelly Thomas's best interest at the time to comply with Officer Ramos's commands. John again went into the different levels of force officers are trained to use, and the different tools or tactics within those levels of force. Baton strikes fell into the intermediate category, as did fists (known as "body weapons"). He then got Smith to agree that a baton is a blunt-force-impact weapon and is therefore a higher level of intermediate force than fists.

Then the zingers. If we've already agreed that utilizing a tactic that had worked previously to deescalate a situation and gain compliance is reasonable, and fists are a lower level of force than a baton, and in the past Officer Ramos had deescalated a situation and gained Kelly Thomas's compliance with the threat of a baton strike, which Smith had agreed had been consistent with training and therefore was reasonable, *then*, if Ramos in this instance sought to deescalate the situation and gain compliance *with a lower threat of force* (i.e., fists) wouldn't that be reasonable too?

It really didn't matter what Smith answered at that point.

In closing argument, John held Officer Ramos' baton in one hand and raised his other in a clenched fist. He raised his baton and rhetorically asked, "Reasonable?" Then raising his clenched fist, looked incredulously at the jury and asked, "Murder?!" The message got across, loud and clear.

General to specific. The Artful Dodger would've been proud.

My cross-examination of Mr. Smith revolved around trial judo: taking what the other side is using against you and flipping it on its head using that same energy or fact/evidence to your advantage. In essence, using the force that's coming against you against your opponent.

In his direct examination, Smith had enumerated eight factors he considered in evaluating if a use of force was reasonable. Without going into each and every one, suffice it to say that all either applied to the actual facts and, more specifically, those facts as seen on the video of the event or could not have been applied based on the specific facts and circumstances. Smith himself testified that only the first factor, officer safety and public safety, applied to every situation. The application of the others, he testified, depended on the facts of the particular case. My cross-exam, then, became a reiteration of his direct exam with the significant exception of utilizing the actual video evidence in the questioning. I'd reminded him of his direct examination, then the specific factor he'd enumerated. I'd even asked him softball questions acknowledging the logic and intelligence of an officer utilizing those factors in the field when assessing a situation that ultimately led to a use of force. Of course, he agreed. I then asked him, hypothetically, if the officer did action "A," would that be consistent with that factor. He had to answer yes. I then went into the specific parts of the video where Jay was demonstrably performing that "action A", pointed it out, and asked him again, with short, controlled questions if what he was now seeing was consistent with that factor we'd just discussed. Again, he'd have to agree, because he already had agreed to the specific hypothetical. To disagree was to look the fool. Every so often I'd insert some questions related to the quickly changing environment, the differences between training and real life. By the time we were done with that section of the cross-exam, Smith had basically agreed that Jay's tactics were letter for letter consistent with *his* eight "factors" he considered in analyzing uses of force.

Another tactic, which I use again and again in use of force cases, is to go over, in detail, all of the materials the use of force expert reviewed, and how many times he reviewed them before coming to his conclusions. I then ask for the amount of time it took for his review. Sixty-plus hours is an average, and the breadth of materials is usually massive—between reports, transcripts, audio interviews, videos, even case law. Sixty-plus hours, stacks of materials. Any expert worth his salt wants to seem thorough, honest, and prudent. Fair. Diligent. Most will say there is no way they would come to a conclusion until reviewing *all* the materials, taking as much time as necessary to be confident in his determination.

My client usually has one, maybe two seconds to decide what is reasonable. The contrast, obviously, is striking (no pun intended).

Which is exactly the point.

Forming the Question

Years ago, I was lucky enough to hear a Minimum Continuing Legal Education (MCLE) tape of a lecture on cross-examinations given by Terence McCarthy, a defense attorney from the Chicago area. It was a multi-hour recording detailing different approaches and styles in cross-examination. My takeaway, which in the last twenty years or more has become a benchmark of my cross-exam style, was to craft many if not most of my questions as short, sharp statements, with my voice rising in inflection at the end to signal to the witness that the statement I just made *was a question*. It creates a quick, crisp rhythm. It keeps the jury involved and interested because of its quick pace. It's a welcome change from the boring and repetitive "Correct?" and "Right?" at the end of most cross-examination questions. And it controls the witness. The witness gets lulled into a series of yes-or-no responses, becoming a puppet and the attorney the puppeteer, which builds your credibility.

It's not hard to do once you get used to it. Just take the question you had planned on asking and break it up. For example, if you're examining the officer in Mrs. Smith's case, you can break up many of the questions into short (sometimes one, two, or three word) questions.

"Officer Nelson, good morning."

"Good morning."

"You testified yesterday that you were called to the front of Ralph's Liquors last August 25 at about 1:30 a.m.?"

"Yes."

"You were dispatched to investigate a robbery?"

"Correct"

"Now, it was one thirty in the morning, right?"

"Yes."

"Ralph's had just closed?"

"I don't know."

"Well, when you arrived it was closed, right?"

"Yes, that's right."

"Now, in front of Ralph's there weren't any streetlights, right?"

"I'm not sure."

"If I showed you a picture of the front of Ralph's Liquors, would that refresh your memory?"

"Sure."

"Showing you what's been marked as People's 2, for identification. Officer, is that a photo of the front of Ralph's Liquors?"

"Yeah."

"Any streetlights?"

"No."

"Refresh your memory that there were no streetlights on August 25 at 1:30 a.m., when you were dispatched to investigate a robbery call?"

"Yeah, there were no streetlights."

"No traffic?"

"Not really, no."

"Early morning hours?"

"Yeah."

"Not many people out?"

"No."

"Safe to say it was dark?"

"Yeah, but I could see ok."

"You parked?"

"Yeah."

"Had your spotlight on?"

"Yeah."

"Because it was dark?"

"Yes.

"Got out of your car?"

"Yes."

"Closed the door?"

"Yes."

"Saw Mrs. Smith on the sidewalk?"

"Yes."

"Walked over to her?"

"I did."

"Contacted Mrs. Smith?"

"I did."

"She was crying?"

"Yes."

"Upset?"

"Yes."

"You used your flashlight to help see her face?"

"I did."

"And the sidewalk, right?"

"Yes."

"That's where she described the robbery happened?"

"Yes."

"It was dark?"

"It was dark—"

"No street lights?"

Smirking, "None, but my spotlight worked pretty well."

"You weren't there when the robbery occurred, safe to say?"

"No, counsel, I wasn't."

"And neither was your spotlight, again, fair to say?"

"Fair to say."

During a federal trial I litigated years ago, both sides had estimated a total of two hours for a key prosecution witness: one hour for direct examination, and one for cross-examination. After the prosecution took an hour and a half, the judge looked at me and stated, "Mr. Schwartz, both sides had originally estimated two hours for this witness. The prosecution went a half hour over their estimate. You have a half hour, then, for your cross." Just like that. He acknowledged that the prosecution had used more time than had been estimated or allotted, but that didn't matter; my cross-exam was still getting the short end of the stick. I looked at the clock, then at my notes and evidence book. A half hour. I launched into a rapid-fire cross-exam, using quick, crisp statements to the witness like I described.

About halfway through, or fifteen minutes into it, I felt I was making progress and scoring points. Then the judge interrupted me.

"Mr. Schwartz," he looked down from the bench. "You've been examining now for fifteen minutes and for the life of me, I don't think you've asked a single question! You're making factual statements, and the witness is agreeing with you. It's very effective, but I'd like you to ask some actual questions." The wind came out of my sails. *He* was the one that had limited my time based on the prosecution going beyond their allotted time. Now that I was using it efficiently and in his own words, effectively, I needed to add the boring mantra "correct" at the end of each question?

It was federal court. And he was a federal judge.

So I did.

For the next several minutes, I added the word "correct" at the end of each question to please him. It worked; he was mollified. After a few minutes, I veered back into my normal approach. By the time he could complain again, my half hour was up. I'd succeeded in eliciting the information and testimony I wanted from the witness in half the time I had planned for.

In some ways, the judge had done me a favor.

DIRECT AND CROSS-EXAMINATIO
Compass Points

. . .

A. Direct Examination
- Leading questions—BORING
- Let the witness tell the story.
- Make it a dialogue.
- Know your facts, COLD.

B. Cross Examination—*Oliver Twist* vs. *Perry Mason*
- Oliver Twist—picking pockets
  - ✓ *General to Specific*
  - ✓ *Forming the Question*
- Perry Mason
  - ✓ *Short, tight, statement-like questions when possible*
  - ✓ *Looping*

CHAPTER SEVEN

TRIAL AND THE ART OF SAILING

I'm not afraid of storms, for I'm learning how to sail my ship.

—LOUISA MAY ALCOTT,
LITTLE WOMEN

Caught in Irons

The summer when my buddy Joey and I emptied our bank accounts and bought a sailboat was probably one of the best summers of my life. Fast-forward thirty-plus years—married, kids, responsibilities. It had been over thirty years since I'd gone sailing. My wife and kids had heard me talk about it countless times and saw old photographs. But the wind, water, and I never quite had time to connect.

Until this past year. While on a two-night mini vacation with my wife in Mission Bay, San Diego, we stayed at a hotel right on the beach with a small, little harbor adjacent. Walking one morning around the beach and grounds, we saw a sign not only for renting boats but also for lessons. I sighed and again reminisced about my sailboat. My wife smiled. "Why don't you rent a boat for us?"

I laughed. "It's been thirty years since I sailed, I'd need a refresher."

"So," she smiled again, "it says they give lessons."

I took out my phone.

We booked a lesson for that afternoon and loved it so much that we booked another for the next day. The instructor, a bearded, weathered thirty-something originally from Massachusetts opined after the second lesson that I was ready to take it out on my own. Enthusiastic, and bitten again with the sailing bug, I bought about fifteen hours of boat rentals at half price. I'd planned on making it almost a monthly Sunday excursion for my wife and me.

About a month later, during my kids' winter break from school, we took the whole family back to Mission Bay. The first full day, one of my sons was under the weather so my wife stayed with him while I took my other kids sailing. We all had a fantastic time. Buoyed by the great day on my own, I took my wife, sister-in-law, and son who'd been a little sick the day before out for a sail the next day. After the lessons the month before, my background thirty years ago, and the previous day's excursion, I figured, "I got this."

There's a sailing term called "caught in irons." Anyone who's sailed, or learned a little about sailing, will recognize the term. It means you've now maneuvered your boat from a good position with the wind (either at 10:30 or 1:30 on the face of a clock) filling your sails, to sailing *into* the wind.

Let that sink in for a moment.

Right.

You *can't* sail *into* the wind.

When this happens, your boat literally goes nowhere and then, worse, starts to go backward. Now, an experienced sailor doesn't let that happen. A less experienced sailor once making the mistake, knows how to quickly get out of it. Truth is, when "tacking" (another sailing term for changing direction by maneuvering the boat into the wind but quickly maneuvering out of it as well), every sailor ends up sailing into the wind. Getting caught in irons means you didn't just sail into the wind for a moment. You got stuck there. Beginner sailors panic, then try to turn the rudder this way and that, never letting the boat right itself, so the sails never get the wind back in them. The more they steer, the more caught they get. They end up working against themselves. Their jib (the front sail) ends up fighting against the main sail (that triangular one in the back). Both should work in unison. But the steering back and forth doesn't allow that. It's like quicksand. The harder you struggle, the more helpless you become.

Well, that second day with my wife, sister-in-law, and son, I got caught in irons. At the harbor we'd rented our boat from, there's a sandbar to the right side when you leave the dock and head into the bay. Trying my best to avoid it, I didn't give myself enough room, and as I started going in that direction, I panicked and tried to turn away from it. Now, I could have tacked and tacked, in effect, zigzagged through it (which I did the day before without realizing it). But I wasn't effectively working my jib so instead of my jib and main sail working in unison, by constantly steering this way and that, they worked against each other. I ended up heading right where I didn't want to go, smack into the sandbar! I called the dock, who sent someone to pull us off.

"You aimed right at that sandbar," the guy in charge that day almost barked at me on the phone when I called for a tow.

Calmly, I defended myself. "I didn't *aim* for the sand bar—"

"I was watching! You headed right into it!" he countered.

He couldn't see my smirk over the phone, but it was there. "I know I headed into it, but I wasn't trying to do that; I *wasn't aiming* for it!"

He laughed. "You needed to let out your main and jib, let the boat swing around, then once the wind catches them, tighten them. You began to tack but never completed it."

The guy who pulled us out of the sandbar added more simple advice. "You always have to have your jib with your main. Whatever side your main is on, your jib is on, unless the wind is directly at your back."

Taking his advice, and implementing it, we had a great rest of the day sailing. When tacking, let go. Let the sails go, so they can switch sides and catch the wind coming across the other side. Then tighten them, and make sure they're working together. Sounds simple. And it is. Once you understand it and know what you're doing.

That mishap probably was the best thing that happened in my renewed sailing career. I now have a much better understanding of what I was doing right, and what I was doing wrong. Hopefully, no more getting caught in irons.

In trial, sometimes you get caught in irons, especially less experienced attorneys. After several trials, there's a tendency to feel like, "I got this." And for the most part, you do. But sometimes things don't go right with a witness, opening statement, or closing argument. The worst thing you can do is dwell on it, or even fight it, by trying to *make* it go right, which is the equivalent to turning the rudder this way and that. Remember, trials have an energy, a life of their own. It's like being on the water and trying to catch the wind. You need to tap into it, feel it.

Connect to it.

Sometimes you need to tack, change directions, adjust. We've talked about that. And sometimes when "tacking," you lose the wind for a moment (i.e., you lose momentum.) Don't panic.

Let the sails out.

Let go.

The wind will come back.

People v. Luke Liu

Luke Liu had been a Los Angeles County Sheriff's deputy for about eight years when on February 26, 2016, he shot and killed a grand theft auto suspect. The suspect, who was trying to evade detention and arrest, made a quick, reaching motion to his right while seated in the stolen vehicle, then popped the clutch, slightly grazing Deputy Liu while the car lurched forward to get away. The shooting occurred at a gas station. The night before, that same gas station had been the location of a gang murder, the murderers having parked at the same gas stall as the suspect Deputy Liu investigated and eventually shot the next day. Both actions—the reach and the car lurching forward—happened nearly simultaneously. Deputy Liu, thinking that the suspect was reaching for a weapon *and* trying to run him over at the same time, fired seven shots into the vehicle. The suspect suffered four wounds, two fatal. The fatal shots were in his upper-left back, just under the shoulder blade and entered at a steep left to right, downward angle. Both bullets ripped through all the same organs, entering the body about two inches apart and resting in the suspect's abdomen, about one inch apart. Nearly two and a half years later, the district attorney filed one count of manslaughter against Deputy Liu. In November of 2018, Luke Liu became the first on-duty peace officer in Los Angeles County in nearly twenty years to be criminally charged for an on-duty shooting.

Seven shots, and the fatal ones in the back, made this an extremely tough case. After examining the surveillance video countless times, which, ironically, did not depict the shooting itself because the shooting occurred behind the gas pumps at an angle not seen on camera, along with the autopsy report, diagrams, autopsy photos, and trajectory rod placements, it became apparent that our defense would have to be in two parts that would meld as one.

- We'd have to convince the jury that, based on the circumstantial evidence from the autopsy, photos, trajectories, etc., the shooting itself happened while the suspect's vehicle was still at the gas pumps, before it began to round the pumps to get away.
- The hand movements in the car, as seen by our client and several of the prosecution's witnesses, would indicate to a reasonable officer on scene that he was in danger of the suspect both procuring a weapon and running him over, making the shooting justified.

In order to do this, each witness would have to be a surgical strike, a pocket to be picked. We needed to get them to either agree or describe (Or not know!) that the shooting happened at the pumps, and that those witnesses who saw the hand movements saw them literally right before and during the shooting. Any variation slightly to the right or left might literally take the wind out of our sails.

The strategy started at the preliminary hearing. If we could "corner" the percipient witnesses into solidly stating the shots occurred in and around the gas pumps, or at least close enough that we can move them there at trial, we'd be in the game. All made statements on the night of the shooting that generally were not so supportive. Their statements did, however, have small details that, if developed, could be supportive of our defense.

The cross-examinations at the preliminary hearing, then, could become the entire case.

They were, or close to it. Building on some of the answers given on direct examination, a combination of developing the testimony needed for trial and surgical strikes (i.e., pocket-picking), we elicited the testimony we needed to make our argument.

All three witnesses the prosecution put on the stand at the preliminary hearing became key *defense* witnesses at trial. Obviously, I don't mean that the defense called them as witnesses. We didn't. The facts we needed the first two witnesses to testify to, that all the shots occurred before the suspect's vehicle had rounded the gas pump, we accomplished. The foundation for trial was laid. The third witness spoke to swift right-hand movements of the suspect just before the car lurched forward and shots were fired. Now we had our details to plug into our narrative, our "big picture." And all of the above was intentionally mixed into the rest of the cross-examination, so it wouldn't stand out too much. It was there, but not flagrantly obvious. Coupled with the circumstantial evidence of the bullet entry wounds, the steep-angled paths through the upper body from left to right, down into the abdomen, we had our argument. The angles, proximities, entry wounds, bullet paths, and now testimonies matched—the shooting happened at the gas pumps. And the cause of shooting?

We'd started with the premise that the client thought he was going to be run over or, more realistically, dragged under the car. But, before the preliminary hearing, we ran a mock jury and, after having twenty out of twenty-four mock jurors convict our client, nearly laughing at that possibility, we almost dismissed that idea and decided to focus much more on the rapid hand movements. So that third percipient witness at the preliminary hearing who saw the rapid hand movements became much more significant.

There's more.

At the preliminary hearing, one of the two witnesses who had stated that the shots occurred before the car rounded the pumps also stated that the chronology/cadence of the shots were first shot, pause, then five to six in rapid succession. He also stated he had not actually seen the first shot, only heard it while stopped at a red light on the street adjacent to the gas station. Upon hearing the shot, he looked up and saw the next five or six. And he also saw the suspect's hands come up in a defensive posture to the suspect's left side, where the driver's door window was, as the shots were being fired into the window. The driver lowered his hands and the car moved forward, and the shots then stopped. Although the prosecutor in his remarks at the preliminary hearing argued that those "defensive" hand movements showed the suspect had no weapon and therefore there was no reason for Deputy Liu to shoot, I had a different take, which I told my investigator afterward and would develop further as we prepped the case, reviewing photos, video, and testimony ad nauseum.

"Put yourself in Luke's shoes, as the deputy on scene," I'd said with a smile. "You approach the vehicle. It starts, and at the same time it seems to lurch forward, presenting a threat, and you see the suspect reach quickly to his right for what you've been trained is a weapon. You fire one shot. The shot that the witness heard but didn't see. The suspect, instinctively, puts his hands up in self-defense. But Luke," I continued, "what *he* sees is one quick hand movement for a weapon, and then a second quick movement that he assumes *is now coming up with that weapon*! So he fires more rounds, where? Where he sees the threat is: those hands at the driver's window. But the car is moving. The suspect is bent forward with hands up to his left side to avoid the gunfire. So those bullets go through the upper-left back and travel left to right, and steeply downward because they're being fired from right outside the driver's window. Even the stray shots that made holes in the car are consistent."

We had our defense, so long as we could keep the witnesses on track at trial in a way that was not only consistent with their preliminary hearing testimony but also didn't require too much memory refreshment or impeachment if their trial testimony wasn't consistent. Some impeachment or refreshing memory is okay. Too much impeachment or refreshing memory becomes boring and tends to alienate the jury. Again, a fine line, but not necessarily a straight one.

Remember, sailing is never a straight line.

There was, however, one last piece of this puzzle that simply jumped in my head one morning during my morning prayers in synagogue. *The shot to the left-front-top of the right knee.* We'd ignored it for the most part, thinking it was the final destination of the through and through in the suspect's left bicep/underarm. Then, while praying, it hit me. *That* shot, really, was the key to *everything*. It wasn't a kill shot. The DA probably ignored it for the most part too. *But it was everything* because it had to have happened first, which means, consistent with the witness testimonies, it had to have happened while Luke was slightly *in front* of the driver, by the driver's mirror! The bullet entered in the left-front of the upper knee and traveled left to right to rest in the center of the calf at, again, a very steep, downward angle. That shot, then, without some real, hard evidence of a ricochet, had to have occurred while Luke was near the driver's mirror, and would be the first shot. And what was next to the right knee? The stick shift, where that first quick right-hand movement would've been if you're the suspect looking to avoid arrest and flee. Luke shot at the hand and hit the knee! Then the car lurches forward, the suspect's two hands instinctively come up quickly in what would've been a defensive posture for the suspect but would've registered to the deputy as the suspect having accessed the weapon and quickly bringing it up to use against the deputy. Hence, the second volley of shots were aimed at the window and the hands but, as the car moves, and the deputy moves to avoid being hit, bullets enter the arm and back, but still traveling left to right, at a steep angle. It all fit.

It had to. Because after the shooting, and after the scene had been investigated and catalogued, about four to five bullet casings were found *not* at the gas pumps, but between the gas pumps and where the car came to a rest, about thirty-plus feet from the pumps, having crashed into the 7-Eleven sign located on the grassy knoll between the gas station and the sidewalk. The prosecution's theory of the case was that Luke continued to run after the vehicle after it rounded the pumps, and he kept shooting. If that were true, then he was shooting while no longer in danger and, if those shots killed the driver, would be guilty of manslaughter. The location of those shell casings, coupled with what we felt was a distorted, uninformed interpretation of the video, supported that theory. And even if we could show the jury that the video interpretation was off, it still didn't explain the shell casings. Therefore, our theory had to be not only reasonable but also charismatic, in a way. It had to "feel" right, not only to us, obviously, but also to a juror.

The surveillance video provided in discovery covered the whole day. We watched the relevant parts that had some connection to the shooting. I won't go into all those details. But the shell casings' location . . .

It would be the prosecution's argument, their entire case. And it was an enigma. We'd have to throw some doubt into the argument that where the casings were found, where the casings had come to rest, was not where they had to have started. Casings bounce. They roll. They get kicked.

And then the video.

After the shooting, the prosecution's video they had planned to use as evidence stopped. Deputy Liu pulls the suspect out of the car, begins CPR, help arrives, and then that's it.

But there was more.

While Deputy Liu is giving CPR, as seen on one camera angle, people begin walking around where the shell casings allegedly were resting, uncontaminated, as seen on the other angle. One person, two, four, eight . . .

A few seconds later, a large black Cadillac Escalade drives through the scene, driving right over where the shell casings were resting, allegedly uncontaminated. The Escalade then stops, the reverse lights on, and it backs up—you guessed it—right over where the shell casings were allegedly resting uncontaminated. The Escalade then drives *forward*, again right over where the shell casings were allegedly resting uncontaminated.

But even with that, there was more. *So* much more.

On the full version of the video, a few seconds later, about a half a dozen deputies ran straight through the area of the gas pumps, where the shell casings were allegedly resting uncontaminated. A few seconds after that, about eight to ten more.

Soon, at the edge of the video screen, you could see the fire engines drive down the street and stage. Moments later about four to six fire personnel, wheeling a gurney, race right through—you guessed it—where the shell casings were allegedly resting uncontaminated. With this, we had a weapon to debunk the prosecution argument that the "pattern" of shell casings was even a pattern at all.

I'd planned on using that part of the video in the closing argument as a surprise. It was also safer that way—to use it with my force expert or another witness might give the prosecutor the opportunity to deflate it with a rebuttal witness or in his case-in-chief, if I were to go over it in cross-exam.

Remember the beginning of the chapter, about beginner sailors being caught in the no sail zone? Experienced sailors might enter that zone, but they don't get caught in it. And after more than twenty-seven years and almost two hundred trials, I was an experienced "sailor."

Spoiler: even experienced sailors make mistakes and get caught in irons.

The witness who'd testified at the preliminary hearing so well to the chronology and cadence of shots—one, pause, then the rest, and the two hands quickly coming up in self-defense, along with the shots occurring at the pumps before the car rounded those pumps—stuck to his testimony on direct. I reiterated it on cross-exam. Surgical strikes, piece by piece. Cross-exam was short, concise, and had gone according to plan. I sat down relieved, satisfied.

The prosecution redirect was messy, seemed unorganized, and insignificant until the second to last question, where the prosecutor squeezed into the question the phrase "While deputy Liu chased after the car," in asking when the shots were fired. Remember "skewing?" Intentional or not, there it was. The witness answered in the affirmative. In reality, he was probably answering "yes" to the timing, location, and order within the question. But I didn't like it; I was worried it would be easily spun in the closing argument by the DA. Against my better judgment, I stood up for recross-exam to "clean up" that one answer.

I entered the no sail zone.

I went back over my first cross-exam to firm up his prior testimony. First couple of questions, no problem. But then I got greedy. I was angling my sails as if my boat would go just because I wanted it to, even though I was about to turn straight upwind. I asked him a question to sum up exactly what I wanted, reiterating the point one last time. But this witness, who didn't want to be there in the first place, had had enough. His shot across the bow?

He qualified what he'd previously testified to and began to add a narrative to support his qualification.

I should've then left it alone. Some damage may have been done, but not devasting. But I was in the no sail zone and began doing what beginner sailors do: fighting my jib against my main sail by constantly moving my rudder back and forth to catch my wind again. What I needed to do is what a sailor should do at this point. Let it go. Before the boat began moving backward or, worse, ended up on a sandbar. Beaching the boat, in trial, might mean losing the case or at least whatever points and credibility I'd scored until this point. I asked him more questions, trying to get him to back off his qualification, to reiterate his cross-examination testimony. But he wouldn't budge. The more I asked, the more he dug in. It became an effort in futility.

When I'd had enough, I finally did let go. But the damage was done. Disgusted with myself, I asked one more insignificant question to at least end looking like I was in control and went back to the counsel table to sit down. My second chair, Nicole Castronovo, whom I was mentoring, looked at me sympathetically. I whispered, again disgusted, "You just learned what *not* to do in cross-exam. Never forget it."

Like in my recent sailing trip, however, I didn't give up or let the mistake begin a downward spiral. The other witnesses went according to plan. We were still in the game. Then came the helping hand, the boat that came and fully towed us away from the sandbar.

Like I've written repeatedly, trials have energy, a dynamic. You can feel it. Connect to it. Momentum. Sometimes a mistake that seems large isn't if you've built up enough credibility, enough momentum; sometimes a small one can seem to take all the wind out of your sails. And then comes a boat to pull you off the sandbar, set you right, and the wind fills your sails again.

Sergeant Gray, now retired, seemed like a small witness. Housekeeping. He was in charge of organizing, investigating, and documenting/cataloging the crime scene. But in the middle of what seemed like standard, boring, mundane testimony came the nugget, the gift from above. The prosecutor, in asking about the shell casings and their locations, also asked if the casings or other evidence can be moved either purposely or inadvertently. "Sure," came the answer, "they can get kicked occasionally." Further questions about their ability to bounce, roll, etc. also elicited similar responses. All, still, somewhat standard. I could go into it more with him about hard surfaces, bouncing, rolling, etc.

Then came the kicker. When asked, the good sergeant testified that deputies are trained to move deftly and gingerly through the crime scene so as not to move shell casings and other evidence. Moreover, he was asked further, if the scene had already been taped off when he got there? Was it previous to his arrival uncontaminated?

When *he* got there . . . ?

Uncontaminated . . . ?

Over two hours after the shooting. Over two hours after people had walked right through the area unobstructed.

Uncontaminated . . . ?

Over two hours after a huge Cadillac Escalade had driven through it, stopped, backed over the same, specific area where the casings had been documented, then went forward and drove over the same area again.

Uncontaminated . . . ?

Over two hours after about half a dozen, then about eight more sheriff deputies ran straight through the area where the shell casings allegedly had come to rest—not gingerly, not carefully—but more like a herd of buffalo stampeding over the plains.

And finally, over two hours after a half dozen firefighters and paramedics, gurney leading the way, ran right through to afford help to the wounded suspect.

I couldn't start my cross-exam quickly enough. "Thank you, Hashem," I whispered with a smile.

My second chair, Nicole, asked me as I stood up to begin cross-exam if I'd planned on using the video. I winked and let out a subtle smirk. She'd read my mind. "Yeah, let's play the video."

Now, during cross-examination of Sergeant Gray, was the time to play the video.

I began the cross-exam by going over mundane facts, reiterating small details. Then came the section with the casings. He readily agreed shell casings, once ejected, can bounce, roll, and most times do. He also agreed therefore it was hard to say with any definitiveness that where casings are found, especially on a hard surface, is where the shooter was standing when he or she fired the gun. I then asked him about the pattern at the scene, and that if those principles in the questions just asked applied to these casings. He agreed, but qualified that the casings here seemed to be in a pattern or grouping and the scene, again, had been taped off and secured.

Uncontaminated.

"That occurred before you got there, right, sergeant?"

"That's correct."

I then asked that if *before* the scene was secured, people were to walk through that area, could those people potentially kick or move a casing, maybe more than one, inadvertently?

He agreed it was possible.

First, I had him authenticate that he was familiar with the investigation, and that he'd been in charge of procuring the surveillance video. Then I had him recognize our exhibit as an accurate, true version of the video he knew had been procured, and that it accurately depicted the events of what it had captured of the shooting and what occurred afterward.

Foundation laid.

We then went to the video.

Each time someone entered the area of the casings, I asked the same series of questions: whether that person or persons could have inadvertently kicked or moved a casing or multiple casings. Each time he agreed it was possible.

It started slowly. In the beginning, it must've seemed that I was grasping at straws. One person, two, three, or four, seconds apart. So what?

But the beauty of that cross-exam was just that it started slow, almost desperate. But it wasn't. I *knew* that video. It would build. And as it built, it would gain momentum.

I let go.

I let the video conduct the cross-examination.

One person walking across the screen.

Set of questions: Could that person or persons have inadvertently kicked or moved a casing, or multiple casings? He agreed it was possible.

Two, then four people moving across the screen.

Set of questions: Again, could that person or persons have inadvertently kicked or moved a casing, or multiple casings? Again, he agreed it was possible.

Then seconds passed.

And then that huge Cadillac Escalade drove through. Right over where those shell casings were allegedly resting uncontaminated. I let the video play until the Escalade stopped. I asked Nicole to pause the video right where the Escalade's reverse lights go on. I had an intelligent jury, and I was betting they could see what was coming.

"Sergeant," I asked, with a lighthearted, curious voice and smile, "did you see what looked like a huge, black Cadillac Escalade drive right through the area that those shell casings were supposed to be, the ones that you logged and catalogued when you got there two hours later?"

He smirked back. "I did, counsel."

I saw one juror almost hiding his face in between his fingers, actually embarrassed to keep looking.

"Could that possibly have moved or changed the positions of a casing or two, maybe more?"

"Sure could," came the reply.

I asked Nicole to play the video. The SUV reversed back, over the casings. More jurors were smirking; some actually shaking their heads. Same questions. Same answers. The SUV moved forward again to the same exchange.

But we weren't done. I let the video play, leaned back against the bar dividing the counsel and jury area from the audience. I relaxed. The seconds ticked by. Then six deputies ran through, right where the casings were.

"Sergeant," I asked, a little lighthearted again, "did you see those six deputies run right through the same general area where you'd catalogued those casings two hours later?"

"I did."

"Now, you testified that they're trained to walk carefully, gingerly, to make sure they don't kick or move a casing or piece of evidence by mistake. But they didn't seem to be walking that carefully or looking out for evidence?"

"No," he responded, "that's when the scene is already secure. Right now, they'd be intent on helping as fast as they could, so they really wouldn't be watching for anything on the ground."

"So, possible one or more of them could've kicked a casing or two, moved it a few inches here, a few inches there?"

"Definitely. Like I said, they're not looking for that. They're looking to help."

More seconds ticked by. Another eight deputies. I shortened my questions to "Sergeant, same questions."

His response, with a smirk, "Same answer."

Two minutes later, the fire engines staged.

When I sat down, Nicole smiled and whispered, "Did you see the jury look at the DA during your cross? They're *pissed*! They know the DA sold them a worthless bill of goods." We could feel the energy, the dynamic had shifted, either back to us or further into our corner.

I could've skipped over parts of the video that didn't have anyone or anything running through the scene. Would've been quicker, less tedious. And much less effective. The video directed that cross-exam. The prosecution's direct exam gave us a perfect opening. I let go, let the wind naturally fill my sails again, and then went with it, directing but not forcing it. The process started, however, when I got caught in irons with the other witness. Had I not been in that situation, making the mistake of not letting go and leaving that witness alone in re-cross-exam, I might not have let go in this cross, with Sergeant Gray.

The prosecutor, himself an experienced trial attorney, at one point also got caught in irons. Our last witness was a use of force expert, Bob Fonzi. I'd used Bob in a few trials and hearings, all with great results. His background and credentials were impeccable: retired undersheriff for San Bernardino County, had run the largest training facility in Southern California, certified in every use of force cadre known to man, trained in martial arts, worked from deputy to undersheriff, was qualified as an expert in both state and federal court. He was intelligent, articulate, reasonable. His direct examination was spot-on.

On cross-examination, the prosecutor pointed out (and I thought he did it well *in the beginning of his cross-exam*) that a timeline chronology of the events that Bob had put in his report was nearly a mirror image of the one in the prosecution's expert's report, which had been written nearly two years before Bob's (before the case was filed). The DA called him on it. At first, Bob wasn't willing to admit it was probably cut and pasted. It seemed to him insignificant; it wasn't his opinions or findings and was consistent with the video. But because Bob wouldn't admit it, the DA kept up the line of questioning, over and over and over again. The judge was shooting me looks to object. I didn't—why should I? He was caught in irons. Fighting not really with Bob, but against his better judgment, against himself. He was obviously alienating the jury. But he couldn't let it go. He'd made his point. More than once. But he wanted that *Perry Mason* moment. So he kept going, fighting with Bob to get an admission that, actually, once it came, was too little, too late.

He'd made a point, but it wasn't as damaging as he'd wanted. He got greedy, he wanted more. He couldn't let it go.

He got caught in irons.

Sailing lesson #1 for cross-exam:

In cross-examination, like sailing, you may have a plan, a direction you want to go, but it's rarely ever a straight line. You need to navigate, feel which way the wind is blowing and catch onto it. Let the wind fill your sails so that it comes across as natural, almost effortless. The effort is in the navigation and working the sails, the big picture (main sail) and little picture (jib) in unison. If your little picture (I didn't like that answer so I launched into a recross-exam I had no need for) becomes too important that it overshadows your big picture (one poor response on redirect really would not have scuttled what we'd gained on cross-exam), your sails aren't working together. You're caught in irons.

Let go. Regroup.

Sailing lesson #2 for cross-exam:

When a boat comes along and pulls you out of irons, take advantage of the opportunity. Let go. The wind is about to fill your sails.

And once those sails *do* fill with wind, make sure you're navigating with that natural wind, not trying to force it. Line up those sails, jib and main. Big picture, little picture. See the help and grab it. Don't force it; go with it.

TRIAL AND THE ART OF SAILING
Compass Points

• • •

A. You can't sail into the wind—Caught in Irons
- Let go
- Don't force it
- Don't panic

B. When the wind comes back, realize it
- Grab the opportunity
- Tighten your sails
- Reconnect

C. Don't wallow in mistakes—learn and overcome them

CHAPTER EIGHT

VOIR DIRE: CONNECT AND PROJECT

We are like islands in the sea, separate on the surface but connected in the deep.

—WILLIAM JAMES

While many a trial attorney may have the opinion that jurors make up their minds during opening statements, I disagree. Voir dire is where most jurors' minds begin to be influenced for or against your case. Voir dire is not just about "selecting" a jury. That may be true for the judge if he or she doesn't allow voir dire (which happens many times in federal court). As attorneys, we all know that no one gets to cherry-pick or simply "pick" the jury. By process of elimination, gut feelings, and most times just choosing the lesser of several evils, juries are selected. For attorneys, then, the purposes of voir dire are really twofold: *connect* with your jury, and *project* to your jury.

A trial attorney is basically a salesperson. His or her products are their case, their clients, and *always themselves*. Like any other salesperson, a litigator has a much better chance of convincing their "customers" (i.e., the jury) of buying their product if the customer connects with the salesperson. In the beginning of the movie *Ruthless People*, Judge Reinhold, a young salesman in a music store, convinces a post-teen couple to buy a pair of six-foot speakers well beyond their price range by cranking the music loud, playing air guitar with the prospective customers, and screaming that the speakers are actually practical because they're so big that "when you die, they can bury you in them!"

Judge Reinhold makes the sale.

So how do we connect, and what do we project?

Connect With Your Jury

Rule one: Be yourself. Every good salesperson either started out believing in their product or, at least, has convinced themselves to believe. A good trial attorney is no different. People connect with self-assurance, confidence, and with people who are *real*. If you are a gregarious person, be gregarious. If you are more cerebral and reserved, be cerebral and reserved (A good, dry, intelligent joke will help show that although you may not be as outgoing as your opponent, you are just as likeable and human.). So, the first rule is to be yourself. If you try to match your opponent's presentation or personality, it will come across as less than genuine. By derivation, so will your case.

You can't connect with anyone in life if you're not yourself. False personas lead to shallow, false relationships. Although, concerning attorneys, Shakespeare wrote, "The first thing we do, let's kill all the lawyers." He also wrote, "To thine own self be true." A trial attorney needs to build a relationship with her jury. Being yourself in front of them, from voir dire onward, means allowing yourself to be vulnerable, real. We wear masks every day in society. Although you won't be divulging any deep, dark secrets to your jury, by being "you," you'll be letting them get to know you, at least a little. And that will begin to build the rapport that connects you to them. It's not a guarantee to win your case, but it's more than halfway there. Unless the product really does sell itself, it's the salesperson who makes the sale. And unless the facts of the case, in and of themselves, really sell themselves, it's the lawyer and her lawyering that really sells the case. Remember, we're trying to evoke empathy, and people can't empathize with someone who doesn't seem real.

So be yourself.

Rule two: Talk with your jury, not at your jury. In voir dire, the attorney is the center of attention. Be a person. Be human. Don't just talk to the jury, talk *with* your jury. If one juror answers a question, ask another juror what he/she thought about the other juror's answer; don't simply restate the question. Spark a dialogue, and be the moderator, but never talk *at* or *to* your jury.

When I was in law school, I had the good fortune to intern for two Washington, DC superior court judges. They were husband and wife as well. The first was the Honorable Zinora Mitchell-Rankin. She had been the third in command of the Washington, DC US Attorney's Office before being appointed to the bench, joining her husband who had been appointed a few years earlier.[43]

Judge Mitchell-Rankin was African American, as was her husband, Judge Rankin, as were both of their staffs. I was the only "white" person working for either judge. It was a great experience on multiple levels, not the least of which was learning from two judges who were intelligent, articulate, honest, and diligent, with very different styles and personalities, and from backgrounds so far removed from mine.

Judge Mitchell-Rankin had gone to undergrad at Spelman College, a Black, all-girls college in Atlanta. She went to law school at GW Law, where I was attending at the time (It was one of the reasons she hired me, along with my previous work experience.). She was a new mother and a conscientious workaholic. I sat in on court proceedings, wrote memos and first drafts of court rulings and orders, researched issues, and had an amazing experience. She was a wealth of information, experience, and common sense.

In the beginning of my tenure, Judge Mitchell-Rankin was on a criminal docket. In DC at the time, the criminal courts were so overwhelmed with cases that trial courts litigated two cases each day: one in the morning, and one in the afternoon. Two trials stand out, to this day, as lessons on how to address a jury.

At some point during the first month of my internship, Judge Mitchell-Rankin was presiding over a drug case in the morning, and an assault case in the afternoon. Both were felonies. The drug case was a possession for the purpose of sales case; the assault was a barroom brawl in which two brothers were accused of assault with a deadly weapon during the brawl. In both cases, the defendants were African American. Both juries were made

---

43 Judge Michael Rankin, who I eventually worked for as well, was later appointed to the DC Court of Appeals.

up of almost all African Americans. Both defense attorneys were African American. In the drug case, however, the Assistant US Attorney (AUSA) was white. In the assault case, the AUSA was African American.

I got to watch parts of both trials, but being that I also worked part time and my internship was for only twenty hours a week (it began as a summer internship and carried over into my second year for credits), I wasn't around for the entirety of both trials. I did see the closing arguments of both, and the verdicts.

In his closing argument, the AUSA in the drug case spoke at the jury, not to the jury. There's a difference. His *demeanor* was *demeaning*, like he was lecturing to a bunch of school children. From their body language and their facial expressions, it was obvious the jury didn't like him. No wonder. From his delivery, it was obvious he didn't respect the jury. The defense attorney, by contrast, spoke to the jury—almost with the jury—as if he were having a private conversation.

In the assault case, it was the opposite. The AUSA was the one having what felt like a private conversation with the jury; the defense attorney seemed too self-confident, almost arrogant in his case.

You might have guessed it. The defendant in the drug sales case was acquitted; the two brothers in the assault case were convicted. Even though they had posted bail, Judge Mitchell-Rankin had them "stepped back" (taken into custody) pending sentencing, which was her standard protocol when someone was convicted of a violent felony. Later that afternoon, we spoke in chambers.

"So," she began asking me. I stood in her office, and she took off her judge's robe, hanging it on a hook. "What did you think of both verdicts?"

I shrugged. "I don't know, I would've thought the opposite was going to happen."

She sat at her desk and smiled. "Your gut is right; the opposite should've happened. So why did the defendant this morning get acquitted, and the two brothers get convicted?"

"I think," I hesitated, "the attorneys blew it."

She smiled again and nodded, "They did!" She leaned forward at her desk. "You're going to be in court in your career, in front of juries. The one in the morning, the drug case, that should've been a conviction. But the prosecutor spoke at the jury like they were a bunch of children, like he was the only intelligent one in the room. He belittled and alienated the jury. To be blunt, he came across as another arrogant white guy. The defense attorney spoke to the jury like he was one of them; he related to them. So they related to him. And their verdict demonstrated that.

"But in the afternoon case, both attorneys were Black," she continued. "So, what happened?"

I shrugged, figuring she really wanted to answer her own question. She did.

"Even though both attorneys were Black speaking to a nearly all-Black jury, the defense attorney was arrogant, too cocky. He should've been able to relate, but again, his arrogance alienated the jury. The prosecutor was down-to-earth, reasonable. He didn't call the brothers monsters, not even bad people. But they crossed a line. He was likable, real, unpretentious. The jury connected with that. And he won.

"Don't ever speak down to juries, don't ever speak at juries." She frowned, shaking her head. "Those brothers could've been home today if their lawyer wasn't so full of himself."

"So," I asked, "why didn't your Honor set aside the verdict?"

It was a law school question asked by a law student.

She laughed. "Unless the evidence just isn't there, it's not my place to second-guess a jury. The standard is, if a reasonable person could convict based on the evidence, not if I would convict. Maybe 'I' wouldn't have," she smiled, "but I'm a judge and seasoned litigator. There was evidence that could lead a reasonable jury to convict. And, unfortunately for those brothers, they did."

Sure, I could've included this anecdote in Chapter One: Know Your Audience. And I could've included it in Chapter Two: Closing Argument. It's applicable really throughout any litigation. So, why here, in voir dire?

Unlike any other time during the trial process, only in voir dire does an attorney really have a dialogue with a jury. Maybe I didn't get to see these attorneys' voir dire, but based on their closing arguments, I could guess the substance, if not the dynamic. Many lawyers make the mistake of either too much explanation, speaking *at* the jury, or not speaking enough. Voir dire is where you begin to build a rapport, a relationship. Relationships are two-way streets; they're about connecting. A successful voir dire is one where the attorney builds that connection.

Talk *with* your jury. You may wax poetic about legal principles and behavioral tendencies, but never stop there. Ask a few jurors what they think about those topics, principles, behaviors, and then ask other jurors if they agree or disagree. Try to start a dialogue between you and the jury, and among themselves. See who agrees or disagrees and why. When one is equivocal, press it. Respectfully, yes, but press it. You're never going to know much about each juror; there's not enough time. But pressing equivocal answers for definitiveness lets you see a few things:

A) Is this juror a sheep? Was the equivocation just a shyness for speaking in public, or a lack of a real opinion, or a reluctance to give one?

B) How do the other jurors react to the equivocal answer, and you pushing for definitiveness? You may be surprised by the overt facial expressions, body language, and sometimes even outbursts of fellow jurors during these exchanges. Part of your overall analysis is not just to focus on the individual juror you're dialoguing with, but also the group as a whole.

C) When informed that the equivocal answer may not be reasonable or acceptable, how stubborn is the juror in his or her opinion or position? Stubbornly sticking to ambiguity may be a trait you don't want on your jury, unless you're hoping for one or two stubborn, emotionally driven jurors.

Pressing for specificity also allows you to keep planting the seed or making the point that you're trying to make to the other jurors (the approach you'd like them to take or the legal or behavioral principle you want to telegraph to them that relates to your case). It also allows you to dialogue with those other jurors about the equivocation, again, making your point, but this time through them.

In a criminal case, when a juror is ambivalent about whether he or she can be "fair or impartial," and answers the question with the abstruse "*I'll try,*" one story I heard years ago from a judge in voir dire illustrates their abstruseness:

Pretend you're engaged, and your prospective husband (or wife) tells you that he is going to Vegas for the weekend with his single buddies for his bachelor party. You say to him, only half-jokingly, "Ok, stay faithful. You're taken, remember?"

His response, "*I'll try.*"

All things considered, would you really be okay with that?

After a few smirks, maybe a chuckle or two, the point is made.

Talk with your jury, not at your jury. Dialogue with your jury.

Rule three: _We trust you._ We talked about this in Chapter 2: Closing Arguments. Voir dire is where you begin establishing that "trust." Most people, even sociopaths (Hopefully none make it on your jury!) want to think of themselves as honest and fair. So, again, like we spoke about in discussing the closing argument, _challenge your jury_. Here, in voir dire. Look them in their faces and tell them that, if selected "_We're trusting you._" Remind them that they will be given a second oath, to be fair and impartial. People tend to rise to the occasion when given the responsibility that someone is putting their trust and faith in them. When we tell people we trust them, the responsibility we place on their proverbial shoulders demonstrates confidence in them. It empowers them; it creates in them a desire to honor that trust. And, consequently, helps them to connect with you.

Project to Your Jury—Planting Seeds

Once you begin to connect with your jury, you can then project. What should you project? Seeds. Yes, seeds. Voir dire is about planting seeds, about guiding a jury on how you'd like them to approach the case, the evidence, and their duties.

Legal Issues. Legal principles are foreign to most people unless they work in the field or have a background. Asking jurors too many times how they feel about burdens of proof and standards of proof they have no experience with, let alone applying, is wasting valuable time and effort. Don't forget, you're asking people to make a decision using a standard very foreign to them. Let them know that. Acknowledge that. It will connect you to them. Then break down those principles into real-life examples, illustrations, and hypotheticals. Connect those real-life examples back to the legal principles in the case. Voir dire is the first opportunity you have to connect the dots between legal principles and real life. You're planting the seeds of how you want the jury to approach their task at hand, the evidence, and eventually a verdict in a way that will speak to them. By connecting to them, you've made the task and forum less foreign, more familiar, whether they realize that intellectually, emotionally, or even subconsciously.

Planting seeds in voir dire is a form of "priming." In his book _Thinking, Fast and Slow_, Daniel Kahneman describes how this effect influences human behavior. The more often certain words or phrases are used in association with a principle or concept, the more the listener or subject will be "primed" to react predictably to those words or phrases in conjunction with that principle or concept.[44]

Planting seeds in voir dire is "priming" your jury for what's to come, to influence them in how to approach the case. It also helps to manage and shape expectations. And expectations guide determinations. Like the mentioned example, the more a juror is "primed" to expect certain facts, legal principles, or behavioral principles, the more they will incorporate those concepts into their thought process and final determination.

Priming can be done by asking the same question, or at least asking about the same concepts to different jurors, throughout the voir dire. A "brand-new" juror or jurors (after some have been stricken already) get a brand-new voir dire, albeit usually a shorter one. As the day goes on, if certain areas are asked about more often than others, whether their patience has worn thin or not (and it will, regardless, so don't be self-conscious; just push forward),[45] the entire room, including jurors that have already been questioned, are being primed, and primed, and primed.

An example I use as a defense attorney is the common, everyday principle of first impressions. Most people quickly have an impression of a given environment or something within that environment. It's part of our instinctual survival mode. When that "first impression" is so dramatic or influential that the person really can't be open to any other impression, I label that person as a "first impression person." Many people are first impression people. And many live very successful lives. I'm not judging first impression people. But when you're a defense attorney, except for voir dire (the one time defense speaks first), the prosecution gets to make the first impression, which could be a serious handicap if a juror is a first impression person.

---

44 For more on this concept, it's highly recommended to read in full Daniel Kahneman's *Thinking, Fast and Slow* (New York: Farrar, Straus and Giroux, 2011).

45 When I see jurors getting tired of the length of the process, I usually acknowledge that although it seems long and tedious, the process is significant, because this is the only chance we have to know how fair and impartial a complete stranger will be. I then reiterate how important the case is to my client, so please, bear with us.

I not only "prime" my potential jurors to expect that the prosecution will make the first impression but do it in a way to let the jurors know that to allow the prosecution to be ahead of the game with that first impression is patently unfair and, in effect, "illegal." I don't use the word "illegal," but in invoking the "legal" standards at work in a criminal prosecution, presumption of innocence and burden of proof, and that throughout the entire process my client is presumed innocent, even while the prosecution is making that first impression. I'm priming them in an implied manner to the concept that to make a determination based on the prosecution case is "illegal," and unfair. I then follow up with why that's so, and why it makes sense. I explain that for a case to even be filed, for a person to be charged with a crime and facing trial, the prosecution case must at least present as reasonable "or we shouldn't even be here." If the prosecution case, on its face, was unreasonable, then my client should not be charged with a crime and in that chair at defense table, and we shouldn't be making all these people—the jurors, judge, courtroom staff, etc.—waste their time for a few weeks. So, they should expect the prosecution opening statement and evidence to at least sound reasonable.

That means reasonableness is the starting point, *not* the finishing line. Just because the government can, and *will*, present a reasonable case doesn't necessarily mean that they've met their burden of proving that a crime occurred, and that my client committed that crime beyond a reasonable doubt. Again, their case should at least make sense, or he should have never been charged. If their case was unreasonable or nonsensical, we shouldn't be here in the first place.

Make sense?

Of course, it does.

And notice the word choice I just used and connected. I associated reasonable with common sense, and unreasonable with nonsensical. I then summarize, without mentioning it, the circumstantial evidence instruction's principles: that the presumption of innocence, coupled with the prosecution's burden to prove guilt beyond a reasonable doubt, means the prosecution's case really should be so reasonable as to exclude any other reasonable interpretation. If it doesn't then, again, should we even be here?

All of the above is broken up into sections. In each section I ask the jurors if that makes sense to them and why. It's an incremental process, broken up to allow for discussion while coming across as intuitive, logical, and natural. Again, not talking *at* or *lecturing* the jury, but speaking *with* them to prime them on what to expect and why.

Factual Issues. The evidence is the facts of the case. We deal with facts in everyday life. Use everyday life examples, then, to telegraph how a jury should view the evidence. For example, if the case hinges on witness credibility, ask questions and use examples of how in everyday life we are routinely called upon to judge credibility.

People love and relate to stories and, by association, to the storyteller. Jurors may have exposure to legal terms and principles through the media, but unless an individual juror has specific experience in the field, that's as far as it goes. When you're inquiring about their understandings or positions regarding legal principles (and their application), bring in real-life examples to get to the point. Rather than constantly speaking to the presumption of innocence, think about mentioning it once or twice but maybe use an example to illustrate the fairness of the concept, either a story of someone falsely accused (in the 70s show *Three's Company*, that was the premise of nearly every episode) or maybe simply asking, "How many people here were ever accused of either doing or saying something that you didn't say or do?" With one real-life question or story, you've made a profound point: a person *can* be sitting in the defense chair and actually be innocent!

Here's where knowing your audience comes in. Whatever you've gleaned of your individual jurors so far, but also, in general, the political, cultural, religious (keep adding adjectives as you see fit) makeup of those jurors, which includes generally the jurisdiction or place/environment they're from, now's the time to apply it. Certain examples, analogies, stories, or even approaches may not go over with certain individuals or groups. Choose your analogies and words wisely based on your audience and personal style.

If there are certain facts in your case that can be emotionally charged, like a graphic video or graphic pictures (autopsy photos in a murder case or wrongful death lawsuit, for example), you may want to address that now in voir dire. If you're looking for an emotional reaction or the opposite, talk about it now. Let the jurors know what's coming.

If the graphic video is to your advantage, meaning that it will shock the conscious of jurors to your advantage, maybe you don't want to mention it too many times, or at all. On the other hand, if you need to diffuse the shock value, then mentioning it at least several times fore-shadows its potentially prejudicial effect. Again, mentioning in a general way some of the specific facts or evidence that the jury can expect manages expectations and allows you to see some reaction before that potential juror is actually sitting on your jury.

If you are looking to diffuse certain evidence, then when you get an emotional reaction from a juror upon questioning, take the oppor-tunity to show that although you're sympathetic, he or she will need to set their emotions aside and decide the case dispassionately based on the evidence, which is not only the fair thing to do, but as the court will instruct them, it's the law. Can they do that? Not only are their reactions important, but so are the reactions of the other jurors listening to your exchange. Even more important is the point you're making.

If the opposite is the case, and the shock value of that diffi-cult-to-watch video or photographs is important to your case, why mention it at all? Let the other side diffuse it; it's their problem. If they do, so be it. If they don't, then once you speak about it or even show it in the opening statement, it may be game over for some jurors. When con-fronted, most people don't admit to being first impression people, but the reality is most people are heavily influenced by first impressions.

Jury selection is the best opportunity to connect with your jury and, resultantly, help them connect with your case. To simply ask, "If you were the plaintiff or defendant, would you want you as a juror?" is to completely miss the point. Voir dire is not about selecting a jury, it's about connecting you and how you approach your case to the jury in hopes that, at the end of the trial, they select you over your opposition with a favorable verdict.

Besides responses to questions, one of the biggest factors to consider is how the jurors are reacting to *you*. Remember, as the attorney, you will be the one doing all the talking during the trial. The jury is your audience. In the closing argument, you will be speaking directly with the jury again. If they're not connecting with you during voir dire or, even worse, are looking disengaged or even disgusted, there's a problem. Little picture is how this individual juror answers questions.

Big picture is planting your seeds, weeding out jurors who have demon-strated they would not be good for you while connecting with them individu-ally and as a group. Establishing that rapport builds that relationship.

VOIR DIRE
Compass Points

• • •

A. Connect With the Jury
- Be yourself
- Talk *with* the jury
  - ✓ *Challenge your jury, but don't patronize your jury.*
  - ✓ *Don't settle for equivocal answers unless the answers tell you what you need to know.*
  - ✓ *Body language—how is the juror(s) reacting toward you?*
- We trust you.

B. Project to Your Jury: Planting Seeds—"Priming"
- Legal Issues
  - ✓ *Wording within jury instructions*
  - ✓ *Approach to their role*
  - ✓ *Procedure/order of the presentation*
  - ✓ *Standard and burden of proof*
- Factual Issues
  - ✓ *Analogize certain facts and principles to everyday life.*
  - ✓ *Use examples from life to illustrate concepts of fairness.*
  - ✓ *Foreshadow explosive or emotional evidence to gauge reaction, minimize reaction, or diffuse certain evidence.*

CHAPTER NINE

OPENING STATEMENT

You never get a second chance to make
a great first impression.

—WILL ROGERS

The opening statement is your first real opportunity to introduce the jury to your case. You may have been able to plant some seeds during voir dire; the judge may have read an agreed-upon paragraph/fact pattern before jury selection. But it's here, in the opening statement, that you really start to put on a case and have the chance to begin to tell your story.

Yes, a story. Whether you're a plaintiff's attorney, a prosecutor, or a defense attorney, you need to tell a story.[46]

"The Evidence Will Show . . ."

If you've had a chance to go see opening statements or been through the exercise in your trial advocacy class, you've heard the phrase "the evidence will show" more than a few times.

---

46 Defense attorneys have the choice of giving an opening statement after the moving party gives theirs or reserving it for before their case-in-chief. I always opt to give an opening statement. Regardless of what jurors claim during voir dire, most people are heavily influenced by first impressions. To allow a prosecutor to give what sounds like a damning opening statement without anything in response, and then straight into the prosecution case is to me, with very rare exceptions, a big mistake.

Boring!

While it may be necessary to use the phrase once or twice in the beginning of your opening, the mantra-like repetition that some attorneys employ, like any other overused phrase, dulls your presentation and tends to lull the jury into a semi-catatonic state. "The evidence will show" is best used as a tool to introduce your opening and then, and most of the time only then, to reuse either when you get an objection that your statement has drifted into argument, or if you sense you're about to get that objection.

If you do get or sense an objection, but don't want to sound boring, just tweak the phrase to fit the evidence, which really means being specific and more detailed. Don't just say, "The evidence will show . . ." Be specific *how* the evidence will show that fact. "You'll hear from Mr. Smith, who will testify to A, B, C . . ." "You'll see a video of the incident that will show/demonstrate/prove/contradict/support . . ." "You'll view medical records documenting . . ." There are all kinds of ways to say "the evidence will show" without actually saying it. Mix it up, be detailed.

But other than that . . .

Tell a Story

Even if you're the moving party and need to at least describe or show the jury the elements you need to prove, address the elements, and then move on. The most effective opening statements are not nuts and bolts rolling around, but stories. Every case is someone's story. Is your client asking for remuneration from a wrongful termination? Or to right a wrong from a negligent medical professional? Are you a prosecutor seeking justice for a victim, even if that victim isn't an individual but society itself?[47] Or are you a defense attorney, seeking vindication for your client? In any of these scenarios, there is a story to tell. Tell it.

Every case needs a theory of the case, whether you call it your theory, story, or drama. It's what the case is about. I wrote about it in Chapter 2 in relation to closing arguments. Here, in the opening statement, is where you introduce the jury to that theory.

Why does it need to be in the form of a story?

It doesn't *need* to be in the form of a story, but in my book (no pun intended) that's the most effective method. Stories, when told well, are

---

47 Although, arguably, even in cases with individual victims, society is a victim as well.

captivating. Stories can also evoke emotions without having to wax into argument, which, again, in opening statements is objectionable.

It may seem obvious, but I've seen many attorneys make this mistake. Don't forget, although *you* know pretty much what the evidence is going to be or the facts of your case, the jury still doesn't. The best, simplest, and most practical way to tell your story, is in chronological order. Quentin Tarantino movies aside, this is not about how creative you can be, it's about how effective. Although there may be witnesses, video, and audio documentation that beg to be addressed "out of order," unless you're really adept at being able to not only hold the jury's attention *and* explain why that piece of evidence is being mentioned now but really doesn't come into play until later, you risk confusing and therefore losing your jury. Make it simple, keep it simple, and make it real. Life isn't a movie or a book; it's linear, chronological with a beginning, middle, and end.

It's Your Stage

With the popularity of PowerPoint presentations in trials, should you utilize one for your opening statement? Juries expect them now, and I can't think of any attorneys in recent years not using PowerPoint for closing arguments. But what about opening statements?

My approach, as a defense attorney, is most of the time I don't use PowerPoints for the opening statement. Now, I was very particular to specify that my approach is directly connected to my role as a *defense* attorney. Were I to have a burden of proof, I might be more inclined to use a PowerPoint in the opening statement, especially to outline the elements I would need to prove and some of the actual evidence the jury will see or hear in my case-in-chief.[48]

So what's the reason *not* to use a PowerPoint? Simple: PowerPoints focus the jury's attention, and any audience for that matter, to the presentation (i.e., the PowerPoint), *not* the presenter. Remember, a huge part of litigation is sales, and the attorney is the salesperson. People

---

48 This especially holds true in civil cases, where through the discovery process and pre-trial rulings the evidence and much of the testimony is not a mystery. It would also apply to state court criminal cases but may not to federal cases where the judges are much stricter about publishing any evidence in front of a jury until a proper foundation is laid in trial.

who have walked into a store without already knowing what they want to buy are heavily influenced by the salesperson; the more likeable, the more connected the buyer feels to the seller, the more likely the sale. *You* need to connect with the jury, to build that rapport. A PowerPoint takes all the attention off you and transfers it to the screen instead. The power of body language, facial expression, eye contact—connecting with another human being(s) is completely lost.

Your jury is not only an audience but also a participant in this morality play. You just finished interacting with them in voir dire. Don't give up that human connection so quickly for an artificial one. In the opening statement, you still need to connect and project, which means you still need to be the center of their attention. So does that mean that you should never give a PowerPoint presentation?

No.

Like I wrote about earlier, if you're the moving party, you may need to use one. Even if you're the defense, you may need to use a PowerPoint. If that's the case, as my wife would say, use it, but don't abuse it. It should be there simply to highlight certain points or to familiarize the jury with certain evidence. When I've felt the need to use a PowerPoint in opening, the slides were general topics or phrases (the name of a witness the jury could expect to testify, for example) or specific pieces of evidence (photographs, video, a business record). I would then describe or expand on what that piece of evidence will be. I didn't spell it all out on the slide. Verbally, in front of the jury, I filled in that blank. I try to use the same style, when possible, in the closing argument, utilizing very detailed slides sparingly so they tend to stand out as important. An example of when to use a detailed slide would be bullet points of testimony that allow you to rattle off a myriad of facts or parts of a witness's testimony while directing the jury to view it. Hearing your voice read off those points will connect you to those points in the jury's memory. It will also highlight the importance of those points because you didn't "abuse" your presentation by putting long, detailed slides throughout; this slide was one of the exceptions, *so it must be important.* The jury needs to be watching and connecting with you, not a screen.

Generic vs. Specific—a Closer Look

How detailed should an opening statement be? There's the incredibly general approach from *My Cousin Vinny*,[49] which, while it may be every defense attorney's dream opening ("Everything he just said is bullshit!"), it wouldn't work in real life to the very detailed approach common to complex litigation like medical malpractice cases, fraud, corporate litigation, certain personal injury cases, etc. The more complex your facts or theory of the case, the more you may need to outline it in detail in the opening statement. It will give the jury a road map and familiarize them with not just the facts, but the complexity of those facts and the case. Without such a road map, the jury may find the case hard to follow and at some point, then, tune it out.

But what if your fact pattern isn't necessarily as complex as a 20,000-page embezzlement case, or a complex medical malpractice case? Do you still give a detailed opening statement?

The answer is, it depends. The more detailed your presentation, the more influential your opening can be. But if there are certain facts that you're trying to surprise the other side with, or inferences that you'd rather not call the other side's attention to at the beginning, you may want to give a more generic opening statement.[50]

The 1977 Denver Broncos

The 1977 Denver Broncos didn't have a roster of superstars, but they made it to the 1978 Superbowl against the Dallas Cowboys, nonetheless. How'd they get there? The 1977 team had talent, yes, and drive, but they also had an uncanny ability to capitalize on their opponent's

---

49 A 1992 comedy starring Joe Pesci, Marisa Tomei, and Ralph Macchio about two college friends driving through Alabama on the way back to school who are wrongly accused of murder.

50 It's safe to say that if you're the moving party with the burden of proof, then it's almost malpractice not to give a detailed opening statement, although you may still decide to keep certain facts or evidence close to the vest rather than put every one of your cards on the table at this point. It's a judgment call that sometimes changes on the fly, depending on the dynamic or energy in the room.

mistakes. Game after game, a fumble here, an interception there, and Denver would turn that unlucky event for their opponent into points for them and eventually win.

That Superbowl, the opening kickoff nearly followed the same script. The Cowboy kickoff return was fumbled near Dallas' goal line, and there was a mad scramble for the ball. One second, maybe two or three passed by. The whistle ended the melee, and a Cowboy player came up with the ball. Guaranteed the majority of those watching, including Pat Summerall, thought (before the whistle blew and it was apparent Dallas had the ball) that it was another example of Denver capitalizing on an opponent's mistake. But that time the Broncos didn't, and you could actually sense that their failure to do so had set the tone for the game ahead. The Cowboys won, 21-10. We all make mistakes during trial—none of us is perfect. Sometimes the differences between a good or competent attorney and a great one, between winning or losing a case, are not letting your own mistakes create a downward spiral, while recognizing and being able to capitalize on your opponent's mistakes.

In the Luke Liu case I wrote about, I was on the fence about how detailed to make my opening statement. On the one hand, we thought there were certain arguments we had prepared that the prosecution hadn't thought of, and if I made a detailed opening statement, it might get too detailed and give away some of our hand. Conversely, our client shot seven times, the fatal shots were in the back, and without a story to hang their hats on, the jury may decide the case right then and there, before any evidence. Although we were solidly set on using the video in the opening, we decided the following: (1) no PowerPoint for the reasons I've stated, and (2) I'd have to thread a needle to make the opening detailed enough to keep the jury impartial, but not so detailed as to give away the farm on those points. I had my notes if I needed them, and Nicole had the video cued up.

And then it happened. Remember the underlying themes throughout this book:

- Know your facts.
- Be flexible enough to go off script when the evidence, or the opportunity, warrants it.

Right before the opening statements, the prosecutor gave me a courtesy hard copy of his PowerPoint presentation, which is standard, professional, and good form. I started thumbing through the pages and noticed that he had taken still frames from his video and inserted captions at the bottom of each, probably about twenty-plus frames. I disagreed with a few of the interpretations of what was being depicted in the frames. Two especially stood out. Both depicted my client near the car the suspect was driving. One seemed to depict him running near the back-left quarter panel of the car, arm extended, as if he were running and shooting at the car well after the car had cleared the gas pumps, which means well after the potential threat had subsided. The second seemed to depict Deputy Liu running right next to the driver's side window with his arms bent, as if holding a gun pointing into the window, again, well after the car had cleared the gas pumps, which means well after the potential threat had subsided. Both captions in each still photo claimed to be depicting Deputy Liu running and shooting into the car.

Two things became more than apparent: (1) The prosecutor planned on arguing that both slides showed Deputy Liu *at different times* running and shooting into the car with no contemporaneous threat, which was therefore unreasonable and, more importantly (2) *the prosecutor didn't realize that the slides he picked were the identical action recorded from different camera angles,* which meant the prosecutor was going to describe and show the jury "evidence" that simply was not true. His version of the edited video was put together in such a way that both angles were never synchronized properly, so where one recording ended, whoever worked on the video simply started the next angle. But the videos had a clock on them that, because the prosecution version had zoomed in, was lost on their screen. Ours wasn't. There was an overlap of the two camera angles for about one second or less that their video missed, which meant *so did they*! I immediately noticed their mistake and jumped on it, playing both them and the judge to utilize their mistake in opening.

Sure, I didn't have my own PowerPoint presentation.

I decided to use part of theirs.

Before the jury came in, I told the judge I'd like to object to the DA's PowerPoint because I disagreed with the captions. The judge shrugged his shoulders and said what any judge would say: "It's their opening. It's what they think the evidence will be. You're more than free to counter that in your opening."

I looked at the judge, purposely almost like a petulant child. "Well, if the court is allowing the government to put on those slides in their PowerPoint, can I use their PowerPoint, too, to counter their opening?"

The judge looked surprised, and a little confused. "You, use their opening?"

"Yeah. The People provided me with a hard copy. I'd like to pull out some of the slides and use them in my opening."

He shrugged his shoulders again. "Sure, I don't see why not. It's just slides from the video, right?"

The DA responded in the affirmative.

"I don't have any problem with that. If they can use it, why shouldn't you?" The judge looked again at the prosecutor. "Any problem with that?"

"Uh, no, Your Honor," was the predictable response.

Like I described in Chapter 2, our version of the video had synched the two camera angles and had both on the screen. I quickly told Nicole to cue up our video to the exact slide that showed both angles of the two DA hard copy slides that seemed to depict, and which I bet would be described by the prosecutor in his opening as two different events/actions (which he did). I then told her that I was going to now improvise the first half of my opening statement, and I'd cue her to play the video. I pulled those two slides out of the prosecutor's hard copy, and several other slides that I now decided to use by putting all of them on the ELMO, the overhead projector. And, finally, those opportunities made me decide to give a very detailed opening statement. I figured that first I would demonstrate the lack of credibility of the prosecution presentation and interpretation, making my detailed opening hit home with the jury that much more. The contrast here, at the beginning of the case, *using their slides*, would build my credibility while instilling doubt and skepticism in theirs. It would become the running theme of the case, which ultimately was the winning theme.

Have an outline, a "script," but don't stick to it. In the Kelly Thomas murder case, in his opening statement the prosecutor put up a picture in his PowerPoint of our client Jay partially on top of Kelly Thomas, Jay's right arm up in the air holding his taser. It was a still frame from the video. The prosecutor went on to describe to the jury that what Jay was about to do was drop that arm and hand, with the taser, as a hammer strike on Kelly Thomas's face. It sounded horrible, monstrous. Problem was, much like in the Luke Liu case described, that really wasn't *at all* what was in that still slide.

The defense team knew that video inside out and sideways. I quickly scrapped the introduction I had planned for my opening and whispered to David (my video expert on that case, too, and many of my cases) to cue up that frame and then be ready to toggle the video to two to three frames before that frame and back. He smirked and did.

When the DA sat down, John Barnett gave his opening for his client. When John sat down, I almost jumped up, chomping at the bit to impeach the prosecutor's opening. We cued up that frame and had it on the screen. I reminded the jury of the prosecutor's claim that the frame depicted my client about to deliver a monstrous hammer strike with the point end of his taser to Kelly Thomas. Then I looked hard at the jury. "Or is he?" I asked, rhetorically. "Please rewind the video slowly a few frames." David did. The jury saw Jay's hand go down toward Kelly Thomas, but not close enough to touch his face, his head, nothing. "Please play it forward again, slowly." Again, David did. What they saw was Jay making circular movements with that same arm to untangle taser wires, *not* ever delivering that hammer strike that the prosecutor had described earlier. We did it again and again, rewinding in slow motion and going forward in slow motion. "That's an example of how this case has been investigated, charged, and prosecuted. And it's an example of why we have trials. The evidence *won't* show that my client delivered a hammer strike to Kelly Thomas's face because he never did. The prosecutor stood up and told you something false. It never happened. Again, that's why we have trials, that's why we have twelve unbiased people from the community to decide. You took an oath. We trust *you.*"[51] Then I segued into the opening statement I'd planned all along.

---

51 Yes, what I said (not calling the prosecutor on his erroneous interpretation) and the way I said it definitely bordered on, if not crossed the line, into argument, but hey, there was no objection. Sometimes you risk an objection just so the jury can hear it, because the jury needs to hear it.

OPENING STATEMENT
Compass Points

• • •

A. **What you expect the facts to be . . .**
- The evidence will show—BORING
- Tell a Story.
- It's your stage—don't play second fiddle to PowerPoints or bells and whistles.

B. **General opening statements—not giving away the farm**

C. **Detailed opening statement**
- The more complex the facts, the more detailed the opening.
- The more detailed, the more influential
- The more detailed, the more risk

D. **Be flexible.**

CHAPTER TEN

CLOSING ARGUMENT, REVISITED

*To be trusted is a greater compliment
than to be loved.*

—GEORGE MACDONALD

Trial attorneys call being in trial "the trenches." Our system is an adversarial one, and trials certainly are battles. Although we discussed the closing argument in Chapter 2, now that we've been "in the trenches," I thought revisiting it, in essence connecting a few dots, would be helpful.

The closing argument is where you get to reap what you've sown from voir dire through the close of evidence. Although you can't rely solely on a great closing to win a case, the reality is that winnable cases are sometimes lost from poor closing arguments. You've laid all the groundwork. Plowed, seeded, and turned over the field. Pick any analogy or cliché you like. Now you need to "bring it home."

Grab the Jury

I stated it in Chapter 2, but it's worth reviewing it again here. Sure, you've obviously prepared a kick-butt closing argument, your preparation beginning when you first got the case (*If* you've been following instructions!). If the beginning of your closing argument is already a grabber, and nothing during the trial has changed that, then fine, go with your preplanned start of your closing argument. But . . .

When I give a closing argument, I like to grab something the other side said in their closing (if you're defense)[52] and knock it down. As a defense attorney, I tell my clients that sometimes the best defense is a good offense.[53]

Think about it. The jury has now sat through the entire trial. Whether it was a few days or a few weeks, they sat, and sat, and sat. They sat through opening statements, they sat through witnesses, they sat through instructions. And now, they're again sitting for your closing argument. Again, don't fall into the trap of thanking them for sitting. It may seem polite, but it's weak. Apologetic. Instead . . .

Energize them.

Empower them.

Now's the time to come full circle with the seeds you planted in voir dire. The legal principles, the life principles, the issues. Remind them of those things. But more than that, now you're free to use, in full force, the evidence and the law that until this point you only alluded to. Don't waste that opportunity. In the opening statement, you began the case by telling the jury your story. Now, in closing argument, you're telling them *how it should end.*

We Trust You

Don't forget to speak *with* your jury at this point, not *at* them. Word choice can be crucial. When you remind them that "we trust you," describe the trial as a journey you've all been on *together*. It's bad form to use the word "I;" what you think is not relevant. It's the facts and the law that count. But here, in the closing argument, you can and should at times use the word "we." It connects you to them, them to you, and all of you to your client and cause.

Remember we spoke about the difference between sympathy and empathy? The closing argument is where you need to really solidify the jury's empathy to your client and your case. "We" does that. Empathy means a person can truly relate to the other person's plight; they can "feel" their pain. Sympathy is fleeting. If all you do is evoke sympathy for your

---

52 If you're the plaintiff/prosecution, then maybe grab something the last witness said. The idea is to start with something that's fresh in the jurors' minds, which, as you'll read above, you'll set up just to knock down.

53 How much more so if you're actually on the offense as a plaintiff or prosecutor.

client or your case, then as fast as that sympathy came, it'll leave when the other attorney has her chance to talk. The people who give a few coins or a dollar to someone in need and continue walking are sympathizing with the person. We all do it. Sure, it's better than nothing. It's easy, quick, impersonal. The people who volunteer in the soup kitchen, for Big Brothers or Big Sisters, raise money for a needy family—they're empathizing. The cause, the people, become part of them. It becomes a "we."

Your case, presentation, argument, needs to evoke empathy. You lead the jury down the path to a place that makes intellectual and emotional sense, but they need to drink from the well themselves. *They* need to own the conclusion. When it becomes theirs, it's personal, and no opposing counsel or fellow juror will move them from that opinion. "*We* trust you" is one of the surest, most effective ways of evoking that empathy. "We all" saw Mr. Jones testify; "We all" read the medical records. Empathy means relating, connecting. They're not going to give you the verdict you're looking for because they need to; they'll do it because they want to.

Challenge the Jury

By telling the jury "We trust you," you're including your client. By describing certain evidence as "We all heard Mr. Johnson," "We all read the medical records," you've now widened that circle to include the jury. You're all connected.

"We trust you" and "We all heard Mr. Johnson testify," serves another purpose as well. It challenges the jury. It implies "You, jury, my client, and I all have a relationship. Don't violate that relationship; honor it." I've argued this overtly when the circumstances allowed it. Sure, it's taking a risk, but all of the closing argument and much of trial is a risk. Any relationship is a risk. That's reality. And there is no relationship without allowing yourself to be vulnerable and giving the other party the opportunity to honor that trust, to respect and protect that vulnerability. By letting the jury know that you are "trusting" them, you're letting them know that you're taking a risk, a very human, personal risk. In effect, you're challenging them to honor your relationship. Most decent people honor a person's trust when given the opportunity. By challenging them with your trust, you're empowering them. People tend to bond with, and feel loyal to, those who empower them.

Take Advantage of Opportunities

Although much of your case was known before you started, during trial lawyers make mistakes. Witnesses testify off script. Things happen that weren't predictable. Even if they were, now that they've happened, you can take advantage of them. If the other side made a big mistake, or if a witness waxed poetic well beyond what you dreamed they would (to your advantage), highlight it in the closing argument. It may be what you lead with, depending on what it was and how it fit into the rest of your case. But whatever you do, *don't* pass over it. Mistakes and fumbles happen in every trial. Witnesses give unexpected presents every trial. Don't be like the 1977 Broncos. Jump on those opportunities.

People v. Richard Heverly

Richard Heverly was a fairly new deputy for the San Bernardino Sheriff's Department when, returning from a weekend excursion with his family to the Colorado River, the 10 freeway heading west was coming to a standstill. About 200 yards ahead, an 18-wheel tractor trailer was on fire in the emergency lane. Unbeknownst to Richard, a tow truck driver had decided to be the good Samaritan and block the number 2 lane (closest to the emergency lane) to help motorists avoid driving too close to the fire. In implementing his plan, however, he drove up the emergency lane and right in front of the Heverlys, cutting off Richard and his family and almost causing Richard to crash into another truck also heading west on the freeway. Obviously upset, Richard regrouped, then slowly pulled up next to the tow truck driver. He took out his flat badge from his shorts pocket and held it up to the window so the tow truck driver could see Richard was an off-duty law enforcement officer. He then waved for the driver to move so traffic could flow, which would create access for emergency vehicles to get through to deal with the truck fire. The tow truck driver, now half outside his truck and on his radio, ignored Richard.

Richard became frustrated. The driver was *not* an emergency vehicle and was now obstructing motorists and, eventually, fire and rescue. He exited his truck and approached the tow truck driver, verbally identifying himself. The driver still ignored him. Richard reached into his truck, his warbag on the dashboard, and pulled out a pair of handcuffs, threatening to arrest the driver and handcuff him if he didn't comply and move the truck. Ignored a third time, Richard reached up, grabbed the driver by the arm and yanked him down from the truck onto the street. A struggle ensued in which the driver reached into the bed of the tow truck. At trial, the driver testified that he was reaching for his cell phone that he'd dropped in the bed of the truck when he was yanked down from outside his cab. He also testified that although he did see Richard's badge, he didn't believe that he was an off-duty law enforcement officer; the tow truck driver himself used to carry a fake badge his uncle had given him and handcuffs for "protection." He assumed, therefore, that Richard was doing the same.

Richard, however, not knowing the driver was reaching for his cell phone, thought he was reaching for a crowbar that was in the tow truck's bed. With his free hand, he reached back into his truck and took out his off-duty firearm, holding it up to the tow truck driver's head and threatening to shoot if the driver didn't stop resisting and comply. The driver stopped resisting, and Richard handcuffed him. He walked him over to the backside of the tow truck and asked him if he took off the handcuffs, would he move his truck off to the emergency lane so traffic, including emergency vehicles, could get through. The driver agreed. Richard took off the cuffs, and the driver moved his truck.

Unbeknownst to Richard, the reason the driver had been so resistive was that he had been on the phone with California Highway Patrol (CHP) when Richard contacted him. Believing, then, that he was already in touch with law enforcement about the situation, he had no confidence in Richard's claims to be an off-duty deputy and, even more so, that he should obey Richard's orders to move the tow truck.

Moreover, as traffic had been at a standstill, several other motorists had exited their vehicles to see what was going on and witnessed the confrontation. CHP received multiple reports of a man with a gun on the freeway. Several officers were dispatched. When the first CHP officer showed up, Richard was wearing his flat badge as a necklace and, walking up to the officer, began to identify himself. The officer quickly asked if he was the man who'd had the gun. Richard answered yes. The officer then walked past Richard to set up cones to help coordinate traffic moving past the area.

Richard was dumbfounded.[54] After a few minutes, the officer came back, placed Richard in handcuffs, and sat him in the back of his patrol vehicle. Three hours later Richard was booked on four serious felonies: (1) assault with a deadly weapon, (2) false imprisonment, (3) battery under color of authority, and (4) criminal threats. At his arraignment he pled not guilty. The first trial resulted in a hung jury. The case was set for retrial.

Although there are points from both trials worth discussing, I want to focus on one event in the second trial that, although seemingly small at the time, ended up being a focal point of my closing argument. One of the percipient witnesses who hadn't testified in the first trial, an older gentleman, testified for the prosecution in the second trial. On direct examination, after beginning to describe the incident, he was asked by the prosecutor if he saw the man who had held the gun to the tow truck driver's head in the courtroom. He testified that yes, he did. The prosecutor then asked him to identify that person by describing where he was in the courtroom and an article of clothing he was wearing. The gentleman then pointed toward the counsel table and said, "He's the gentleman next to the prosecutor, wearing the police uniform." He had pointed out the investigating CHP officer, not my client!

The jury began to snicker.

A little flustered, she asked again, that maybe he'd been confused by her question. But he was firm. He pointed his finger right at the investigating officer in uniform, and again described him by his position at the counsel table and his uniform. The jury's snickers turned to quiet laughter. This time the prosecutor got up, walked behind my client, and asked the question one more time, subtly pointing in front of her. But the older

---

54 During the cross-examination of the CHP officer, I got him to agree that being dispatched to a "man with a gun' call on a crowded freeway was probably one of the most dangerous situations he could confront as a peace officer. I then piece by piece questioned him about, having been dispatched to what he had agreed was the most dangerous situation a peace officer might face, upon arrival he decided to ignore the man with the gun, and instead lay down traffic cones! Then, every so often during the cross-exam, I'd remind him of the gravity of being dispatched to a "man with a gun" call, and his decision to ignore that same man with a gun, opting to direct traffic instead. You guessed it—a form of looping. After the cross-exam was over, he couldn't get off the stand quickly enough. Another nugget for my argument: Richard, a.k.a., the "man with the gun" was not a threat, but a professional, which is why the CHP officer instinctively prioritized traffic control over securing an "armed suspect."

gentleman wouldn't bite. He firmly identified the CHP officer at the prosecutor's counsel table. The jury laughed. She stopped asking the question.

Me?

"*Leave the gun. Take the cannoli.*"

No questions on cross-examination.

I already had my nugget. Why risk tarnishing it?

In the closing argument, besides highlighting that based on my client's training and experience the reach for the cell phone would have been interpreted by my client as a highly dangerous movement by the tow truck driver, I reminded the jury of the misidentification. "Why did Mr. Smith firmly, repeatedly, insist that Officer Jones was the man with the gun on the freeway, and not my client? Aside from both being white, they don't look alike." (The older gentleman was Caucasian too.) I paused and then leaned into the jury. "Officer Jones was in court during the whole trial *in uniform*. Mr. Smith wasn't identifying a person, he was identifying *a uniform, a persona*. He was basically testifying that the man with the gun, my client, Richard Heverly, had been acting like a cop, a trained professional. And try as she might, the prosecutor couldn't drive that image from his mind or from his testimony. My client wasn't committing a crime; he was acting consistent with his training as a first responder, as a law enforcement professional. He wasn't in uniform that day, but in the eyes of Mr. Smith, he might as well have been. He was performing his duties."

We won the case. Sure, there were other witnesses who *did* identify my client as the guy in the shorts, T-shirt, and flip-flops who'd had the gun pointed at the tow truck driver. And there was much more to the case and my argument than Mr. Smith's misidentification. But the impression made by Mr. Smith's testimony rang true. Remember, trials have energy, life. I used his misidentification as my grab to begin my argument, to set the foundation for my theory of the case. I again mentioned it at least twice in the body of my presentation. Sure, I could've mentioned it to simply argue the unreliability of Mr. Smith's testimony. I could've maybe mentioned it once as a reminder of the levity it created within the prosecutor's case. But it was worth more than that. Much more.

After the acquittal, the jury waited outside the courtroom to speak to us. As soon as we exited into the hallway, they surrounded us. Two hugged Richard. More than a few shook my hand. It was obvious that we'd connected with them.

CLOSING ARGUMENT, REVISITED
Compass Points

• • •

A. **Grab the Jury**
B. **We Trust You**
   • Reconnect voir dire with closing
   • Jury needs to *own* their determination
C. **Challenge the Jury**
D. **Take advantage of opportunities from the evidence and opposing counsel's closing.**

CHAPTER ELEVEN

STORIES

But how can you live and have no story to tell?
—FYODOR DOSTOYEVSKY

I wrote about the use of stories in Chapter 2. Stories are a great way to convey a principle or argument in closing argument; stories also provide for great analogies in voir dire to discern a potential juror's opinions and positions on certain concepts, legal principals, and approaches to life.

I love stories. I tell stories at my Shabbos table. When my kids were younger, I would make up characters and their ensuing adventures while putting my kids to bed. Stories are with us from childbirth and throughout our entire lives. They allow the listener to not only relate to the story and storyteller but also to connect with him. Not many things make a point or engage an audience like a good story.

Below are some examples of stories I've used over the years.

Joseph and the Coat of Many Colors

I used to utilize this story in the closing argument when the prosecution's case hinged on circumstantial evidence. It's a story most people all know and therefore can relate to. Although biblical in origin, it espouses no particular religion or belief. It also makes the point well. One judge, after hearing me tell it in the closing argument, called me to the bench after the jury began deliberations to tell me how much he liked the analogy.

We've discussed in voir dire that in a trial, you're asking the jury to utilize a standard of decision making that is foreign to them. Things can be suspicious. The prosecution's case can, on the surface, sound reasonable (see our previous discussion on the circumstantial evidence instruction). But is it proof beyond a reasonable doubt?

Jacob's first and true love was Rachel. But before the wedding, he was duped into marrying her sister, Leah. Back then, a veil was really a veil, and he couldn't tell the difference until after the wedding. Although he woke up angry (smirk and wink) he couldn't have felt **that** *violated as he had seven kids by Leah, four more by two other wives, and finally two by his love, Rachel.*

Rachel died while giving birth to her second child, Benjamin. Joseph, her older son, became Jacob's favorite among all the brothers. He doted on the boy, spoiled him. The brothers became jealous and began to hate Joseph. At one point, Jacob gave Joseph a coat of many colors. It was the most beautiful coat in all the land. And Joseph, being the spoiled teenager, flaunted the coat. "Look what dad gave me, isn't it awesome?!"

That was all the brothers could take.

So, one day, when Joseph was sent by his dad to fetch his brothers from the field, they took him and ripped the coat off his back, looking to kill him. But Ruben, the oldest brother, spoke up. "We can't kill him," he chided. "He's our brother! Throw him in the pit for now. I need to go to the field; when I come back, we'll decide what to do with him." They threw him in the pit, and Ruben left.

But throwing him in the pit wasn't good enough. They could hear Joseph screaming to be let out. After an hour or two, it got to them.

A caravan of traders came by. Judah had an idea. "Let's sell him to the Ishmaelites! We're not killing him, but we are getting rid of him!" The brothers, their hatred still seething, agreed. And Joseph was sold into slavery, down to Egypt.

Ruben came back to find Joseph gone. Frantic, he asked almost screaming, "Where's Joseph?! You killed him?!"

"NO!" came the resounding retort. "We agreed not to, remember?"

"Then where is he?" Ruben almost cried.

Judah spoke up. "Don't worry, he's alive. We sold him to the Ishmaelites heading down to Egypt."

Ruben almost exploded. "You did WHAT?! You sold our brother into slavery?! What's wrong with you?! What are you going to tell Dad?"

The brothers stared at each other. "We didn't think of that." Then they had an idea. They took the coat they'd ripped off Joseph's back, tore it some more. Then they killed a goat and dipped the torn coat in the blood. They took it to their father and showed it to him.

"Is this your son Joseph's coat?" they asked.

Jacob grabbed the coat and screamed, "My son! My son! He must've been killed by a wild animal! My son, my son!" Hugging the coat, he couldn't be consoled until over twenty-two years later . . .

Now for the jury:

"We all know Joseph wasn't dead. We all know he was really sold into slavery in Egypt, went through a lot trials and tribulations, finally becoming the second in command of Egypt. And we all know how it ends.

"Sure, four hundred years later there's Charlton Heston, Yul Brynner, and the *Ten Commandments.*

"But what about Jacob? If you look hard at the "evidence" he had in front of him, it seemed reasonable that he thought his son was dead, eaten by a wild animal. Such attacks were prevalent back then. And he had the coat, torn, covered in blood. Three thousand years ago there were no DNA tests, no blood tests. Even more, his other sons were the ones who presented the "evidence" to him. Why would he think they had any bias? Why would they lie?

"But they did. Or, at least, didn't present the whole truth. If Jacob had looked more closely at all the evidence, he may not know that Joseph was sold into slavery, but he certainly would've had a reasonable doubt that he was killed by some wild animal.

"Had Jacob examined the coat better, he would've noticed that yes, there was blood, but where was the evidence of human remains? Had a wild animal ripped into Joseph while he was wearing his coat, there'd be pieces of skin, flesh, maybe even hair on the coat, both human and animal. But there was none.

"There'd be a doubt . . .

"If Jacob had then decided to investigate further and go to the last place Joseph had been seen—the well—he would have seen signs of a struggle, but not of a struggle between a man and beast. He would've seen signs of a struggle between man and man. No signs of human flesh, bones, animal prints. Only human prints.

"If Jacob would have examined the coat, if Jacob would have gone to the well, he may not know exactly what happened to Joseph, but he'd certainly have a reasonable doubt that he was dead, killed by an animal. What started out seeming reasonable based on the evidence, in the end wasn't.

"Jacob would have a reasonable doubt.

"Ladies and gentlemen, here we are, at the end of the trial. The People have given you a coat, a theory, and asked you to convict. We're asking you to look closer. It's no coincidence that this place, here, is called the "well" of the court. It's the place where the case unfolded in front of you, where the evidence was presented. The prosecution wants you to look at this case on the surface, to accept their argument at face value. Don't make the mistake Jacob made. Examine the coat; examine *all* of the evidence. [Here, insert an example from your case of a fact or facts that seemed damning on the surface but, in fact, turned out to be the opposite or, at least, benign.]

"Go to the well. You've taken an oath to be fair, impartial, to hold the prosecution to their burden of proof. We trust you to do just that. Because if you do examine all of the evidence objectively, there is only one verdict you can come to. The evidence supports it; justice demands it. Not guilty."

The Wagon Driver[55]

Negligence

In a small town there lived an old wagon driver. He'd been the only wagon driver for that region for many years and now, having grown old, had decided to sell his business, his horses, his wagon, and retire.

He put up some signs in his town and two neighboring towns that he was selling his business and would be "interviewing" potential buyers. Within a few days, he had at least half a dozen young to middle-aged men showing up at his door, offering good money for his business. What they didn't expect was being examined by the seller. Prospective buyer after buyer failed the tests.

One enterprising young man answered question after question to the old wagon driver's satisfaction, and surprise. Things were looking up. Finally, a buyer.

---

55 Based on a story told by HaRav Ephraim Wachsman

Then came the last question. The old man smiled and started slowly.

"Let's say you're driving the wagon with a few people, and you run it into a ditch. Wheels dig in. What do you do?"

"Well, I'd whip the horses real hard," he answered, "driving them real hard, until they pulled the wagon out."

The old man smiled a soft smile. "Okay, let's say you do that, and it doesn't work. What do you do then?"

The answer came without hesitation. "Well, I'd rip some planks off the wagon, put them under the wheels for better traction, take off some of the bags to lighten it up, drive the horses hard, and pull it out of the ditch."

The old man rubbed his chin and took a sip of his coffee. "Okay," he continued, "that makes sense. Let's say you do that. And it doesn't work. Then what do you do?"

Again, the young man shot back, without hesitation. "I'd get the people off the wagon. I'd ask the men to push from the back, and I'd whip the horses hard, and between the horses pulling, the men pushing, the wood under the wheels and less weight on the wagon, we'd pull it out of the ditch!"

"And if that doesn't work?"

The young man looked more than confused and stumped. "I really don't know, then."

The old man leaned forward, shook his head. "Sorry, but you don't pass the test." He leaned back and took another sip of his coffee.

Frustrated, the young man got up to leave. He stopped at the door. Turning, he furrowed his brow, put on his hat, and looked the old man in the face. "Alright, fine. Test or no test, if you don't want to sell me the business, that's your choice. But let me ask you. I gave you every possible approach there is, and you still said I was wrong. What IS the right answer?!"

The old man rubbed his head. "You know, I don't know either. But I DO know that a good wagon driver doesn't drive his wagon into a ditch in the first place!"

For the jury:

"Ladies and gentlemen:

"If Mr. Smith were as cautious and careful as he claims, this case never happens. If he were really driving a speed that was safe for the road conditions, there is no accident. He had a duty of care. He had a responsibility to be prudent, responsible.

"A good wagon driver doesn't drive his wagon into a ditch. He's paying attention. He's trustworthy. Driving is a privilege in this society, and no privilege comes without responsibility. A safe, prudent, conscientious driver is aware of the road conditions and adjusts accordingly to be safe, not just for himself, but for everyone, including my client. Mr. Smith drove his wagon into the proverbial ditch. He wasn't being cautious; he wasn't being vigilant. He was driving too fast for the road conditions and now, my client is irreparably harmed. Mr. Smith didn't act responsibly that night. He needs to take responsibility now. That's why we're here. That's what you're here for. That's why we have juries. We trust you. Hold him accountable. The evidence supports it; justice demands it."

The Cage in the Hut

It was my first few months as a licensed attorney. I'd just started as a vacation relief in the Ventura County Public Defender's office. One of the senior attorneys told me I should go watch Todd Howeth give a closing argument. Todd was a senior felony attorney. Blond hair, tall, well-spoken, and well-read, he was extremely articulate and poised. I was told it would be good training.

It was.

The client was charged with felony assault with a deadly weapon causing great bodily injury for a fight that broke out at the beach. He'd taken a baseball bat and beaten another young, twenty-something. The defense was self-defense: the client claimed that the "victim" was a gang member who had attempted to rob and assault the defendant's younger brother.

When the defendant came to his brother's defense, a real fight broke out. Todd's client asserted that the victim had threatened him with the bat first, but his client was able to wrest it from the victim's hands. There was also evidence adduced that Todd's client had been an associate gang member. Tough case.

I didn't see any of the evidence, only the closing argument, and not even all of that. But what I did catch, the following story, stayed with me for years. Thirteen years, to be exact. Somewhere in the back of my mind, my psyche, I was waiting for the right case to use the story (although I tweaked it to make it mine and fit the case).

Ivory Webb was that case.

In Northern India, a person can hire a guide to take them through the jungle to a designated location away from the city. Not near any particular village, not near any real civilization. The trip is on foot and takes a few days, could be up to a week, in the jungle. The guide has a machete, and day after day he cuts the vines and branches on a trail only he knows, through the sweltering heat. Humidity drips from the trees; mosquitoes swarm all day, all night.

Finally, after a few days in the heat, the vines, the mud, and the bugs, you come to an opening in the trees. It's a small opening, and in the middle is a hut, and it's a small hut. It's round, made of mud-bricks, with a mud grass roof. It's actually not much bigger than the well of this court, where I'm standing right now. If you look closely, there's no door to get in. Your guide points to the ground. A hole, leading to a tunnel. He motions for you to crawl in. You do.

The tunnel is small; it's a squeeze, but you crawl and squeeze for what seems like forever, the dirt and mud surrounding you, worms, bugs. Finally, you feel a slight change in the air. The tunnel begins to go upward, ever so slightly. You crawl up and climb out of the hole. You're now standing in the hut.

Looking around, the hut is small on the inside just like it looked on the outside. Small and empty except for a table right in the middle with a cage resting on top. There's a bird inside the cage. Above the cage, you notice a small hole in the roof of the hut. A small ray of sunlight pushes its way through the hole in the roof and into the hut.

The cage has a door, which is locked. On the table is a key. The key fits the lock.

The week of heat, sweat, mud, and vines, mosquitoes, and thirst.

The dark, cramped, dirt-packed tunnel.

This is what you came for . . .

To take the key.

Open the door.

Set that bird free.

To experience the thrill, the joy, of setting another being free.

For the jury:

"Ladies and gentlemen, we've been through the proverbial jungle in this case. Weeks of cutting through the vines and leaves, the evidence presented. Crawling through the mud, the dirt in the tunnel. And now, here we are. At the end of the trial.

"In the hut.

"And make no mistake, my client, Ivory Webb, is that bird. He's been waiting for *you*. An unbiased, impartial jury.

"He's been in that cage for over a year. But you have the key. You can unlock it. There are two verdict forms. They say "not guilty" on them. They're the keys.

"Soon I'll sit down, and the prosecutor will address you in his rebuttal argument. Don't forget what we've just talked about when you go back to deliberate.

"Go over all of the evidence.

"Apply the law the court gives you.

"Then take those keys.

"Those two verdict forms.

"Unlock that door.

"Open the cage.

"Set him free.

"Let him finally go home to his family.

"End this nightmare.

"The evidence supports it.

"Justice demands it.

"Take those keys.

"Not guilty on both counts. Thank you."

Stories can seem trite, but if told well, stories evoke emotion. Stories connect people to the material; they connect people to the storyteller and, in trial, to your client.

An experienced sailor connects with his surroundings, becoming part of the sea, the sky, the air, while at the same time, remaining apart. Just like in sailing, so it is in trial.

And in life.

Bibliography

Hill, Napoleon. *Think and Grow Rich*. New York: Ballantine Books, 1937, renewed 1988.

Kahneman, Daniel. *Thinking, Fast and Slow*. New York: Farrar, Straus and Giroux, 2011.

CPSIA information can be obtained
at www.ICGtesting.com
Printed in the USA
BVHW050837290323
661355BV00012B/298/J

9 781662 931239